A BRIEF HISTORY OF

WYANDOT COUNTY OHIO

A BRIEF HISTORY OF

WYANDOT COUNTY OHIO

RONALD I. MARVIN JR.

on behalf of the Wyandot County Archaeological and Historical Society

THE History PRESS

Published by The History Press
Charleston, SC 29403
www.historypress.net

Front cover, top: A circa 1970 postcard view of the current Wyandot County Courthouse, erected in 1900 at a cost of $199,740. *Wyandot County Historical Society*; *bottom*: A group stands on the Stepping Stones that were used by Wyandottes and early settlers to cross the Sandusky River. *Wyandot County Historical Society.*

Back cover, top: A group of local men pose for a picture near the original Colonel Crawford Monument in the late 1800s. *Wyandot County Historical Society*; *bottom*: An early 1900s hand-tinted postcard showing the Indian Mill with the original dam over the Sandusky River and the fish ramp. *Wyandot County Historical Society.*

First published 2015

Manufactured in the United States

ISBN 978.1.46711.768.5

Library of Congress Control Number: 2015941433

This book is dedicated to my parents, Ronald and Annie Marvin, who have steadfastly supported me throughout my archaeological and museum career.

Contents

Acknowledgements

I would first like thank the board of trustees of the Wyandot County Archaeological and Historical Society for its support in this project and for providing unlimited access to research materials, documents and images. Aside from certain photographs I took specifically for this book, all of the images used in the book are from the Wyandot County Archaeological and Historical Society photographic and document archives. I need to extend a special thank-you to all of the donors who have graciously provided historical materials to the society since its inception.

I want to thank the staffs of the Upper Sandusky Community Library, Dorcas Carey Public Library and the Mohawk Community Library for their assistance in researching this book, including providing access to records and microfilm. I am indebted to the researchers and authors of previous articles and books that provided much background and historical information. The websites I visited during research are too numerous to mention, but a few I consulted regularly for dates and to corroborate information are Ancestry.com, Google Books, the Wyandotte Nation websites, Library of Congress Newspaper Archives and, of course, Google Search to send me in the right direction

Individuals I need to recognize are Charlotte Leeth, who shared many historical stories and loaned me her notebook full of county history articles; Tom Hill, who took me on my first tour of Wyandot County historical sites and monuments; Jean Moon, Nancy Sauer and Betsy Bowen, who told me many stories about the Wyandotte Indians and the Mission Church;

Dan Shields, Erin Bartlett, Sarah Logston, Betty Brown and the staff of the Ohio History Connection, who offered support at the Wyandot Indian Mill; Wyandotte chiefs Billy Friend, Norman Hildebrand and Ted Roll, who shared stories about the current Wyandotte Nations; my fellow curators Janet Engle, Brittany Molnar, Robin Conley and Cassie Carlson; Bonnie Eyestone and Katherine and Minette Hull, who gave unwavering support of my local historic efforts; James Gatchell and Sara Lou Binau, who detailed historic stories about the area; Don and Nancy Bower, who were sounding boards during research; my parents, Ron and Annie Marvin, who listened to my excitement when I found new and unique historical information; and Krista Slavicek and the staff at The History Press, who provided me this opportunity. I also need to thank everyone I have encountered during my time as curator at the Wyandot County Museum: you are the reason for sharing this brief history.

INTRODUCTION

When writing a book like this it is extremely difficult to condense several thousands of years of human habitation and development into a little less than two hundred pages. There are definitely hundreds of historical items and stories I had to leave out and others that I could only briefly mention. Local museums and historical sources in the bibliography detail many of these missing stories.

The tale of Wyandot County goes back thousands of years to the first inhabitants following the last ice age. Until the emergence of European traders and settlers, numerous native tribes hunted and lived in this part of northwestern Ohio. Of all the native tribes living in the Ohio Territory, the Wyandottes are most associated with our county. Where they once had free reign over the entire state, they had been restricted to two small reservations in or near then Crawford County by the early 1800s. In 1843, the Wyandotte Nation, the last of the native tribes to live in Ohio, was moved west to the Kansas Territory.

The U.S. government formed Wyandot County in 1845 from former lands of the Grand Reserve and surrounding counties. Early pioneers moved into the county, cleared land and drained marshes—preparing it for future settlement. Growth in and around the former Wyandotte town of Upper Sandusky resulted in its incorporation in 1848. Several other towns sprang up around the county (Carey, Nevada, Sycamore, Marseilles), which aided in its growth and prosperity.

By the late 1800s, railroads had replaced wagons on the Indian trails and plank roads as the primary mode of transportation. The first ones arrived in the 1850s and soon crisscrossed the county. When the young automobile industry took hold, carriage makers began to work on "horseless carriages," and Upper Sandusky even hosted its own car manufacturer. The year 1913 witnessed the birth of the coast-to-coast Lincoln Highway, which ran east–west directly through the county. As air travel became more common, the county established its own airport.

Military service has been a common theme from the formation of the county. Beginning with the volunteers of the Mexican and Civil Wars to the draftees of World War II and Vietnam and continuing with the current volunteers in the armed forces, Wyandot County's residents have answered the call of duty. Memorials to these brave men and women can be found in towns and cemeteries throughout the county.

Weather- and transportation-related disasters were all too frequent as well, including the Great Flood of 1913, the blizzard of 1976, numerous train wrecks and the crash of Lake Central Airlines Flight 527. Firebugs struck early on, leading to the formation of local volunteer fire departments that continue to the present.

Wyandot County has also been home and host to international actresses, professional athletes, nationally known companies, *The Shawshank Redemption*, the Liberty Bell, Charles Dickens, Wyandotte chiefs, Ohio governors, U.S. presidents and even the first man to walk on the moon. There are several historical sites, monuments, memorials and museums in Wyandot County to visit that will enhance and illustrate the stories contained within this volume. It is through connecting with our past that we can illuminate our future. This was an attempt to highlight Wyandot County's history for current and former residents, plus those with a love for the past. I hope you enjoy reading it.

1

Prehistory of Wyandot County

The story of the area known today as Wyandot County goes back thousands of years. The last ice age vastly altered the land, smoothing down hills and leaving large packets of brackish water that eventually formed marshes and bogs in the area. Located on the edge of the Great Black Swamp, one of the better-known marshes was the Cranberry Bog in the northeast section of the county. Glaciers scoured the land, leaving huge piles of stone, gravel and other assorted debris as they receded. These kames and eskers featured prominently in the earliest occupation of the area.

As the Wisconsin Glacier slowly exposed the land, new species of plants and trees grew in the area creating a new climate for native inhabitants. The wildlife quickly adapted to this unfamiliar terrain, and the native peoples found themselves hunting unfamiliar and varied animal species. This new environment would have supported only a handful of hunters and gatherers as they adapted to the new environment.

As railroads expanded through Ohio and surrounding states in the late 1800s, tons of stone were needed for the railroad beds. Numerous quarries opened in Wyandot and surrounding counties to fill this need. The easiest stone to acquire in the early days was from sand and gravel pits, known as kames, dotting the region. Workers soon discovered a curious addition to the stone. Skeletal remains of early native inhabitants, along with lots of grave goods, were buried in the stone. Students in the young field—at least in Ohio—of archaeology began to examine the remains located in the kames to better understand them. They were soon named the Glacial Kame

Culture, which according to archaeological evidence was predominant about 1000 to 700 BC.

These natural geological features were used as cemeteries by nearby groups and could contain hundreds of burials placed over numerous generations. Similar sites have been recorded throughout northwest Ohio as well as Indiana, Michigan and Ontario, Canada. Despite the presence of the cemeteries, no permanent structures or villages have been definitely associated with the Glacial Kame Indians. Archaeologists estimated that each cemetery might have been associated with a particular clan of roughly fifty to sixty persons. As there are three known cemeteries in Wyandot County, the population living in the area during this period would have been about three hundred persons.

The three known sites associated with the culture have been discovered about five to seven miles apart along the Sandusky River. Cemeteries at the Thomas Reber, Cherokee Ford and Pipetown sites have provided valuable clues about how the culture lived. The most well known is the Thomas Reber Glacial Kame Site, which archaeologist Edward Galitza excavated extensively from the 1930s to the 1950s. He meticulously recorded his work, which was written up in professional journals, including several issues of the *Ohio Archaeologist*. His work produced conclusive evidence of this culture's burying its dead in the area. Several artifacts discovered during his excavations at the Reber site are currently on display at the Wyandot County Museum.

Archaeological investigations throughout modern Wyandot County have revealed the presence of numerous habitations over several thousand years. The *Ohio State Archaeological Atlas* recorded fifty-three mounds, eighteen burials, eight villages and one cemetery in Wyandot County. Native tool-making debris and projectile points can still be found by collectors and amateur archaeologists in the area. Work at a site just south of Upper Sandusky revealed the presence of Late Archaic peoples (3800–1700 BC). Additional excavations have revealed the presence of early Woodland groups inhabiting the region roughly five hundred years ago.

Archaeologist Ken Clark surveyed and excavated a site near the lower end of Broken Sword Creek. Known as the Clark Locality, it has yielded hundreds of stone tools, points, scrapers, bifaces and other associated artifacts dating from 7200 to 500 BC. They cover the Archaic and Woodland periods. Many of the excavated items are on display at the Wyandot County Museum.

During the Woodland era, new cultures arose and utilized the land at least for hunting, as very few early dwelling sites are evident in the archaeological

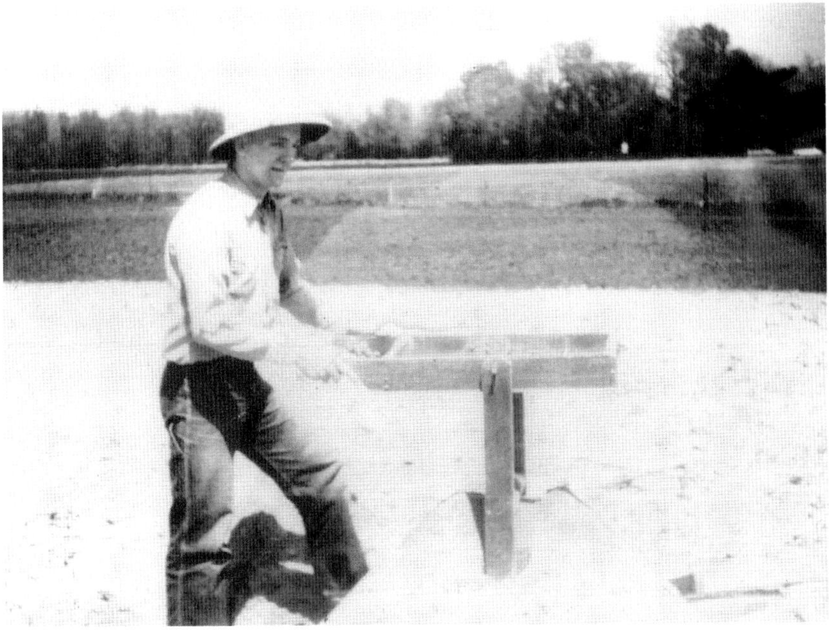

Archaeologist Edward Galitza uses a dirt shaker screen during excavations at the Thomas Reber Glacial Kame Site in the 1950s. *Wyandot County Historical Society.*

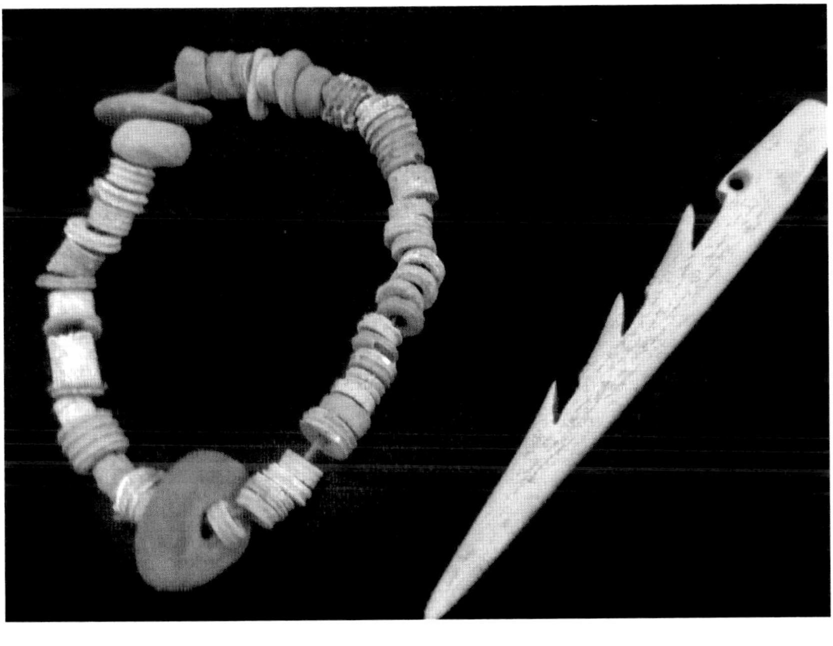

Glacial Kame shell and crinoid necklace (1955) and bone spear point (1933) recovered from archaeological excavations at the Thomas Reber Site. *Wyandot County Historical Society.*

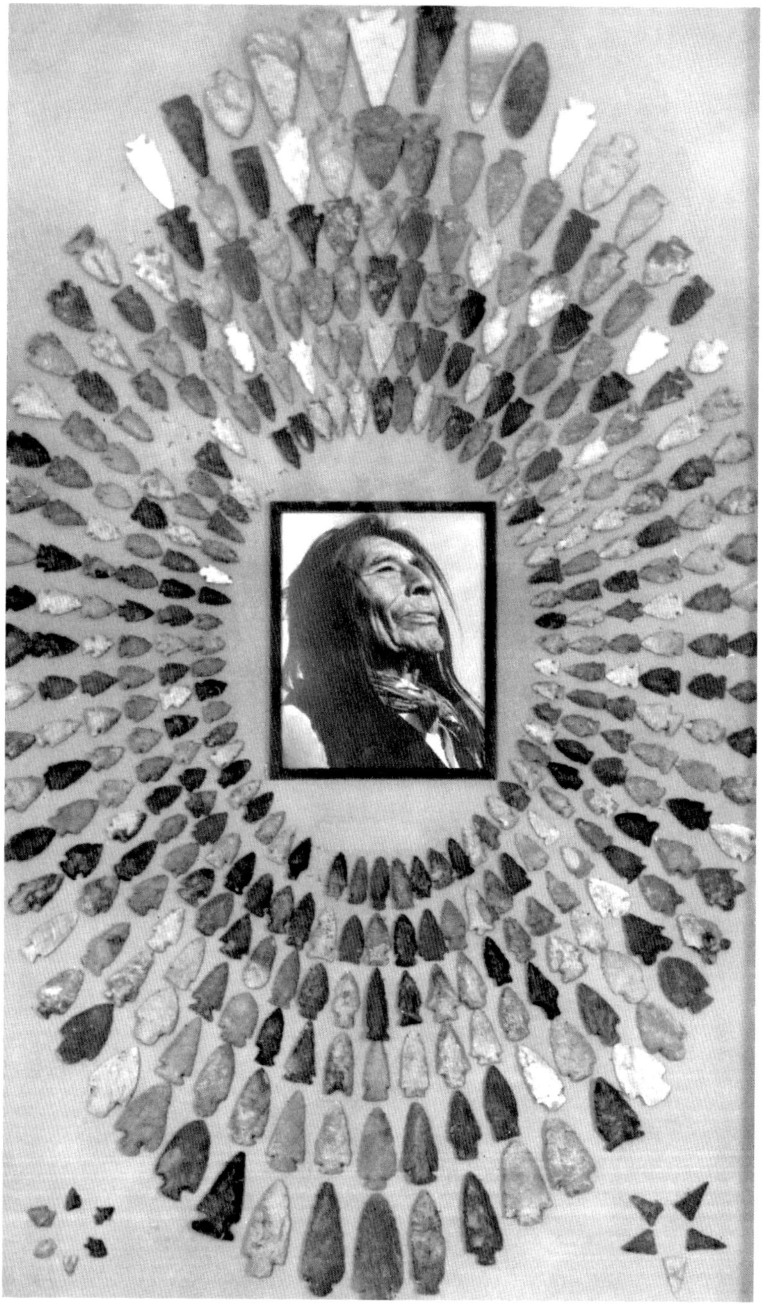

Assemblage of projectile points discovered throughout Wyandot County currently on display in the Wyandotte Room at the Wyandot County Museum. *Wyandot County Historical Society.*

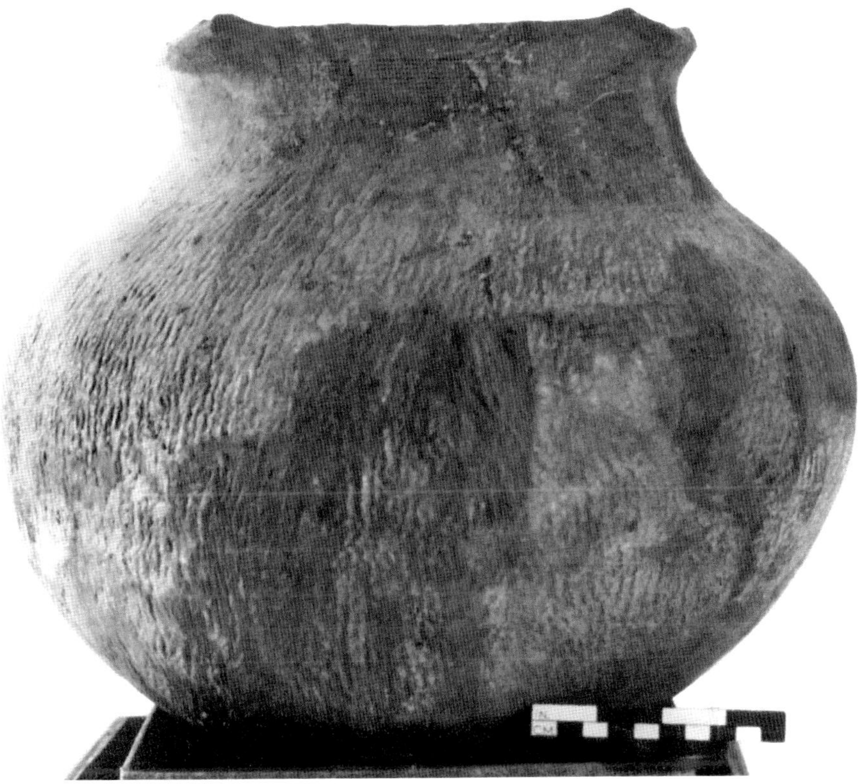

Image of a Late Archaic period ceramic vessel discovered along the Sandusky River in Crane Township by Frank Tilton and Chester Martin. *Wyandot County Historical Society.*

record. One of the greatest collections of archaeological materials comes from the Lower Broken Sword Creek near Nevada. Adena (700 BC–AD 1) stemmed blades were found in the area, as well as stone tools in the Hopewell (AD 1–500) style. A large site southwest of Upper Sandusky produced large amounts of projectile points, ceramic fragments and blades from the Hopewell period. Blades from this period were also discovered near Sycamore. Early Late Woodland (AD 500–800) projectile points were found in the vicinity of Marseilles.

In addition to the human habitation, the paleontological record shows evidence of a wide variety of animals that roamed the region. During the Archaic and Woodland periods there was an abundance of wildlife, including elk, bears, wolves, mountain lions, woodland bison and smaller game, such as beavers, bobcats, otters, porcupines and rabbits. Birds, such as the passenger pigeon, prairie chicken and sandhill crane, could be seen flying

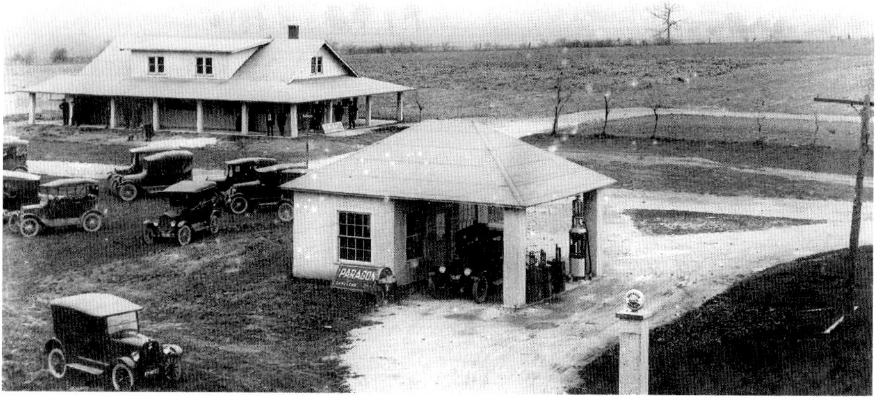

A circa 1926 postcard showing the original buildings constructed over the entrance to the Underground River Cave, currently the Indian River Caverns. *Wyandot County Historical Society.*

overhead at one time. Much of the paleo-fauna information was gleaned from excavations at the Sheriden Cave site associated with the Indian Trail Caverns in the northwestern section of the county.

The Indian Trail Caverns are located northwest of Carey along a natural limestone-dolomite ridge containing one of the largest cave networks in the state. Originally discovered in 1926, the Underground River Cave was owned and operated by Mr. M.L. Kelly. Unlike most caves, it lacked colorful limestone deposits and cave formations yet still attracted curious visitors due to its unusual natural skylights. Kelly installed electricity in the cave and constructed a shelter house over the entrance prior to opening the site to guests in 1927. It was later renamed Indian Trail Cave because it was believed to be part of a network of caves visited by local Indians, including the Wyandottes. The so-called Indian Council Chamber ceiling has cave drawings, which were found during archaeological excavations in the 1990s.

By the 1980s, the Hendricks family had acquired the tourist site. While cleaning out a sinkhole in 1989 to look for passages that might expand his show cave, Dick Hendricks discovered another sinkhole, which he named the Sheriden Cave for the original owner of the land. During excavations between 1989 and 2000, over fifteen thousand cubic yards of sandy soil was removed from the "Sheriden Pit."

From 1990 to 1995, paleontologist Dr. H. Gregory MacDonald of the Cincinnati Museum of Natural History conducted excavations revealing the presence of numerous late ice age mammals. Skeletal remains of over

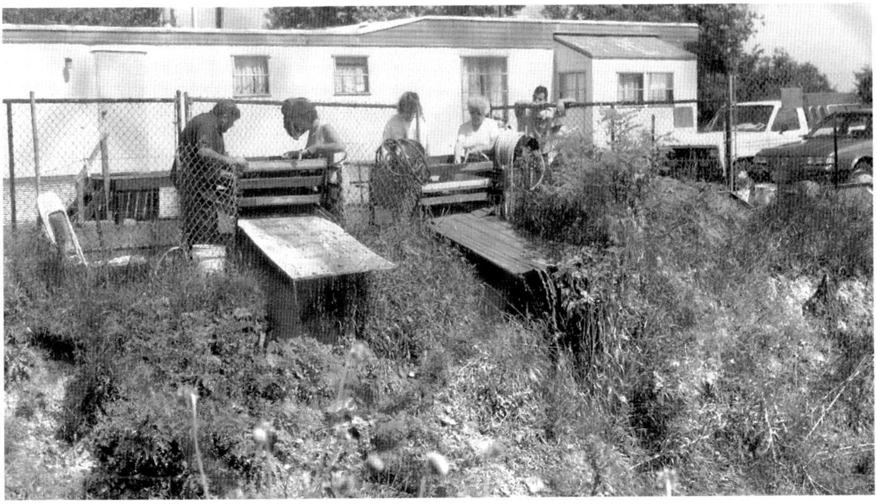

Volunteers use water hoses and screens to sift through dirt and other materials recovered during archaeological excavations at Sheriden Cave in the 1990s. *Wyandot County Historical Society.*

sixty-five species were recovered, including bats, voles, flat-headed and long-nosed peccaries, snapping turtles, giant beavers, stag moose and the short-faced bear.

Once human evidence was discovered in 1996, archaeologist Dr. Kenneth Tankersley from Kent State University took over the investigations, conducting additional excavations until 2000. He was assisted by students from Kent State University and volunteers from the Cleveland Museum of Natural History. Among the many Paleo-Indian specimens found were two bone projectile points, plus the oldest in-situ Clovis-type point found in Ohio. Over twenty-five radio carbon dates were taken from this site, dating it sometime between 11,000 and 10,500 BC.

The project quickly became world famous, and the site has been featured in numerous television shows and documentaries. In August 2001, the Ohio Historical Society erected a historical marker at the site. The Indian Trail Caverns continue to be open to the public during the summer months with guided tours focusing on local archaeology and geology.

Interestingly, according to local archaeologists, the population of Wyandot County remained stable until about 1200 BC, when almost all the population left this region and headed north to villages along the Sandusky Bay. It is unclear why the natives left the area after nearly 2,200 years of habitation. It would not be until the late 1600s that evidence of native peoples

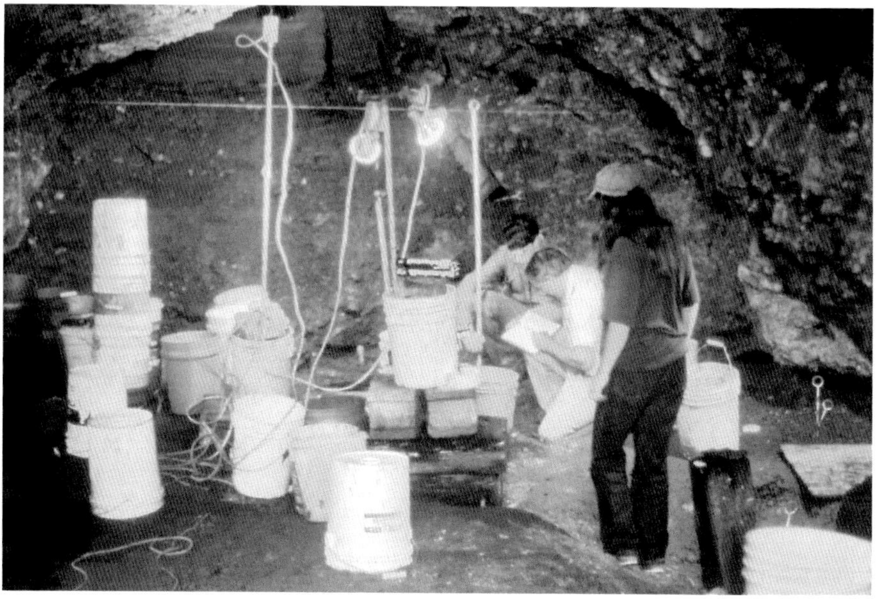

Archaeologists and volunteers take a break to record artifacts unearthed during excavations at Sheriden Cave near Carey in the 1990s. *Wyandot County Historical Society.*

inhabiting modern-day Wyandot County appeared in the written, oral and archaeological records. Historians finally began to encounter documented inhabitation of the region in the 1700s.

Numerous indigenous nations were living in the Ohio region at this time, and it was relatively peaceful, with each group having its own hunting lands. Hunters followed the game and set up temporary camps as needed with a few permanent villages dotting the landscape. It was not until the arrival of the Europeans that tensions began to rise and the course set for these hunting lands to become the Wyandot County we know today.

Between 1805 and 1843 federal government surveyors kept intricate notes regarding the land and vegetation in each section. These descriptions were later merged onto Government Land Office Survey Maps. While the land may differ from what Archaic residents encountered, the Ohio maps from 1818 to 1843 give viewers a glimpse into the landscape encountered by the Wyandottes. The Middle Sandusky Drainage Basin was primarily a prairie covered by various trees, such as oak, elm, ash, hickory, maple and beech. The lands west and northwest of Tymochtee Creek tended to be wetter and marshy as compared to the rest of the county. At least four cranberry marshes dotted the region (two near Wharton and two near Upper Sandusky).

2

Settling the Ohio Territory

Following a fierce conflict with the Iroquois Nation, a new Wendat Confederacy was formed in 1649–50. The new nation moved south from Canada into what is today southern Michigan and northern Ohio, settling on the Sandusky Plains. Being one of the oldest nations in the Ohio Valley, it was considered the "grandfather" nation and its opinion and/or permission was usually asked before other nations acted in the area. There were occasional battles between nations, but as the Americans began to expand and increasingly encroach on their lands, the Wyandottes joined other native groups to fight off the new threat.

In 1782, due to an uprising of native warriors in northern Ohio following Colonel David Williamson's massacre of the Moravian-converted Delaware village at Gnadenhutten, Colonel William Crawford was coaxed out of retirement by government officials, including his old friend George Washington, to lead the American soldiers sent west to break up the uprising. Selected leader of the men over Colonel Williamson by five votes, he led the Sandusky Campaign from May 25, 1782, to June 12, 1782. Its goal was to destroy native towns along the Sandusky River and end the numerous attacks on settlers. Crawford and Williamson led about five hundred volunteer soldiers, mostly Pennsylvania militia.

Heading into present-day Wyandot County, the troops encountered the natives in an area now known as Battle Island north of Upper Sandusky on June 4. Essentially an ambush, British and Indian warriors surrounded the Americans and took minimal losses while over seventy Americans were killed.

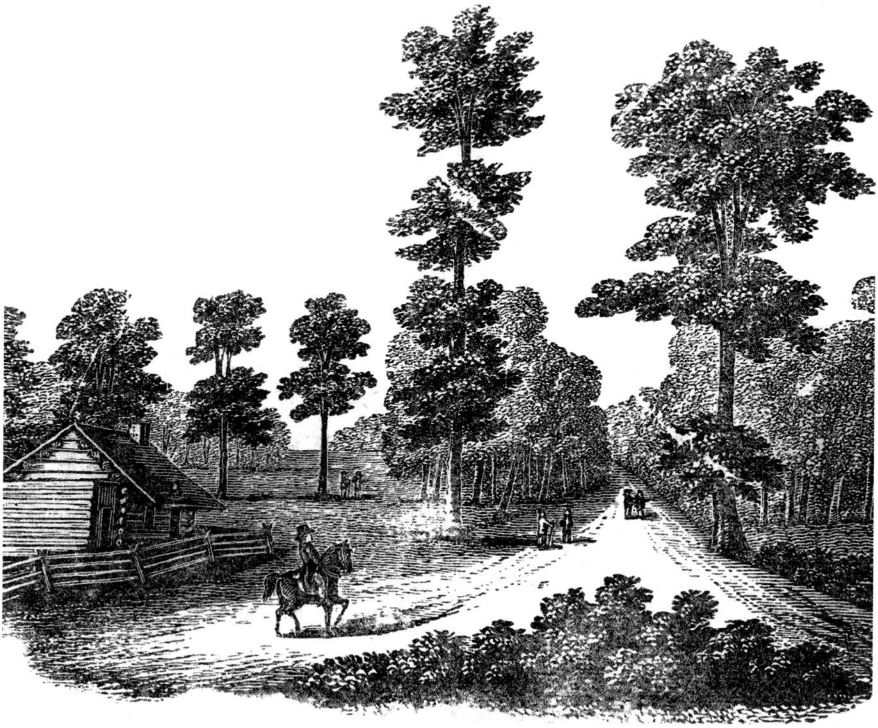

Sketch of the 1782 Battle of Sandusky Plains site north of Upper Sandusky prepared by Henry Howe in 1846. *From* Historical Collections of Ohio, *1891*.

Chaos soon broke out, and many of the Americans retreated. Williamson's men engaged the natives the next day at the Battle of Olentangy and were driven out of the Indian Territory.

On September 19, 1926, the Battle Island Monument was dedicated along the western edge of current State Highway 67. The small brick column was erected by Tarhe Tribe No. 145 of the International Order of Red Men to commemorate the nearby battle between Crawford's forces and the native inhabitants. According to historian Ray Gottfried, the inscription was actually carved on the back side of an old, illegible tombstone from the area.

During the Battle of Sandusky Plains, Colonel Crawford and several men were taken captive. While most were executed almost immediately, Crawford and Dr. John Knight were held for execution. Captain Pipe, leader of the Delaware Nation, demanded Crawford's public execution as retribution for the deaths of the Delaware at Gnadenhutten, even though he was not

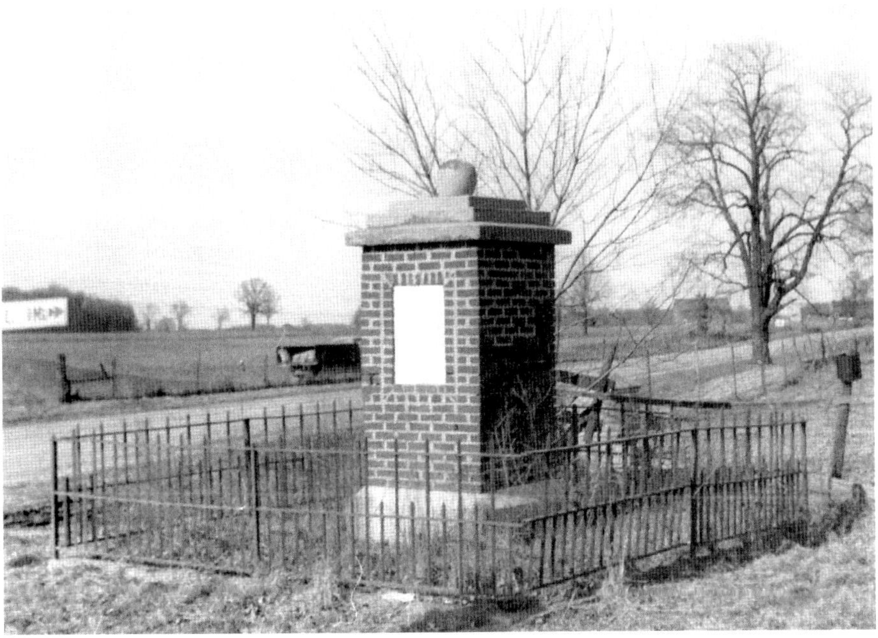

A 1957 photograph of the Battle Island Monument erected by Upper Sandusky's Tarhe Tribe No. 145, International Order of the Red Men. *Wyandot County Historical Society*.

directly responsible. At Nine Oaks, an Indian council was quickly held, at which Crawford was sentenced to death. On June 7, Knight and Crawford were taken to Captain Pipe's Delaware camp along Tymochtee Creek. Their faces were painted black, the traditional sign indicating that a prisoner was to be executed. After a brief conversation with Chief Wingenund, Crawford was stripped and bound in preparation for his execution.

Dr. Knight was forced to watch as Crawford endured horrific torture over several hours prior to being burned alive at the stake on June 11. Knight managed to escape the next day during the trip to a nearby Shawnee village for his execution. Following three weeks in the wilderness, he finally reached an American settlement and relayed his horrific story. This encounter only inflamed tensions along the frontier between the Americans and Indians, leading to armed conflicts throughout the next forty years.

Colonel William Crawford was born in 1732 in Berkeley County, Virginia. He grew up with and was a lifelong friend of George Washington, both trained surveyors. He served as an ensign in the Virginia Riflemen during the French and Indian War and as a captain in the Pontiac War. Crawford settled in western Pennsylvania in 1767, becoming a justice of the peace.

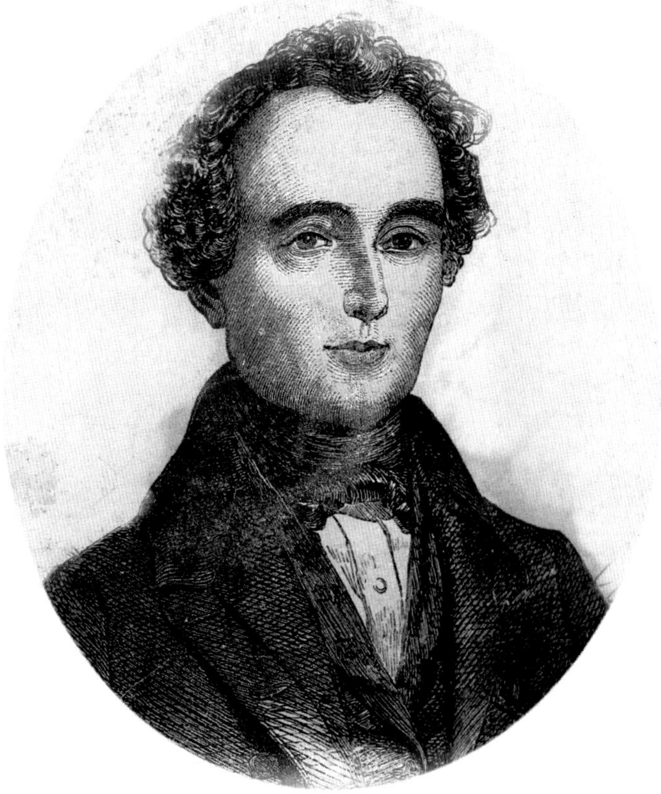

A circa 1880s cabinet card etching based on original family paintings of a young Colonel William Crawford, who led the somewhat ill-fated Sandusky Campaign. *Wyandot County Historical Society*.

When the American Revolution broke out, he enlisted a company of men from Virginia and was promoted to lieutenant colonel of the Fifth Virginia Regiment. In 1776, he was promoted to full colonel and later participated in the Battles of Long Island, Trenton, Princeton and Philadelphia. He was assigned to the frontier in 1788 and soon occupied himself with quelling the Indian attacks on western settlers. Following twenty-five years of military service, Crawford retired to his farm to spend a peaceful retirement. However, in May 1782, at the request of George Washington and William Irvine, he accepted the leadership of the expedition to suppress the native attacks along the Muskingum and Sandusky Rivers in Ohio, a fateful mistake.

He died a horrible death on June 12, 1782. His remains were reduced to a pile of bones and ash whose exact location is unknown. Only a handful of people, including his widow, ever saw it, and no permanent marker was ever placed on the burn site. The two monuments erected in 1877 and 1994 were placed in the general area of his execution.

In 1792, General "Mad Anthony" Wayne was named commander of the U.S. Army of the Northwest Territory by President George Washington and tasked with protecting settlers along the frontier from Indian attacks. Following several attacks and minor skirmishes, in August 1794, Wayne led his troops from their fort at Roche de Bout. After marching for a while, the soldiers approached the Maumee River. They finally encountered the massed natives at the Battle of Fallen Timbers, named for a group of trees knocked down by an earlier tornado.

Anticipating the soldiers' arrival on August 19, the natives fasted before the battle in keeping with their traditions. When Wayne's troops finally arrived on the twentieth, the Indian warriors, led by Blue Jacket of the Shawnee, were weak from hunger. Despite trying to use the felled trees as cover, they were quickly defeated. This was a devastating engagement for the natives, as every nation took heavy casualties and nearly every chief there was killed.

It was said that the Wyandottes fought valiantly that day despite being pinned down. However, it came at a heavy price, as twelve of their thirteen chiefs died with only Chief Tarhe surviving. He was severely wounded in the right elbow and took several months to recover. Sensing the might of the soldiers and the power of their government, Tarhe began to advocate for peace with the Americans. He decided to take whatever measures were necessary to ensure the safety and security of the Wyandotte Nation.

Following this defeat, most native leaders knew that they would have to seek peace or risk annihilation by the American Army. Beginning in January 1795, representatives from both sides met at Fort Greenville, Ohio, for eight months to discuss terms of a treaty. On August 3, 1795, General Wayne met with a large gathering of native leaders to finalize the treaty. The recognized leader of the Indians was Chief Tarhe while his son-in-law Isaac Zane was the primary interpreter. Following a lengthy and passionate speech, Chief Tarhe became the first Indian leader to sign the Treaty of Greenville. As keepers of the Calumet (a ceremonial peace pipe), the Wyandottes were entrusted with the Indians' copy of the treaty.

Representatives of the Wyandotte, Delaware, Shawnee, Ottawa, Miami, Eel River, Wea, Chippewa, Potawatomi, Kickapoo, Piankashaw and Kaskaskia Indians signed the treaty, which gave all the northern lands, including present-day Wyandot County, to the native groups living there. The nations agreed to relinquish all claims to the lands south and east of a

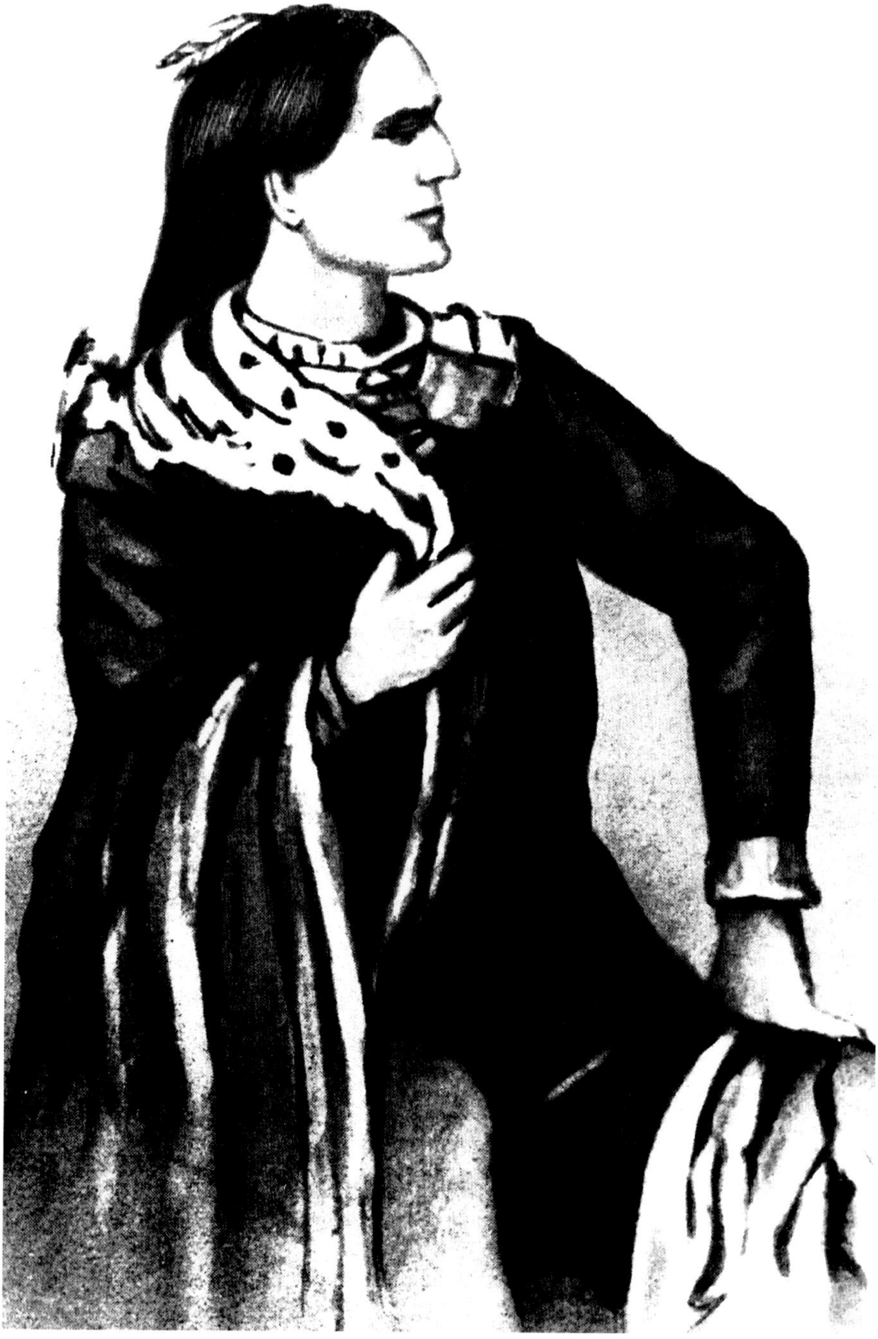

Sketch of Chief Tarhe (1742–1818), leader of the Wyandotte Nation during the signing of the Treaty of Greenville in 1795. *Wyandot County Historical Society.*

boundary line that began at the mouth of the Cuyahoga River, hence southward to Fort Laurens, westward toward Fort Recovery and finally southward to the Ohio River. The treaty provided accommodations for the natives to continue to hunt on the land they ceded. Even though the treaty forced the Americans to relinquish their claims to the lands north and west of the aforementioned line, the natives allowed several small trading posts to be established in their territory, as this was beneficial to both sides.

Chief Tarhe was born about 1742 near Detroit, Michigan, to a Wyandotte mother of the Porcupine Clan. His name is very unique and has been interpreted various ways. In the Wyandotte language, it reportedly meant "the tree" or "at the tree." He was nicknamed the Crane by the French due to his great height (six feet, four inches) and slender build. The English, not having a suitable translation, soon adopted this nickname. Early on, Tarhe opposed white settlement of the traditional Indian lands of his forefathers. He participated in numerous battles as a young warrior, including the Battle of Point Pleasant (1774) under the Wyandotte chief Chiyawee and was near the Battle of the Thames (1812) when Tecumseh was killed.

The sachem was the head of the Wyandotte Nation and carried the title of Sastaretsi. In 1788, Tarhe was selected to succeed Too-Doh-Reh-Zhooh as sachem, the first member of the Porcupine Clan to hold the title. He last fought at the Battle of Fallen Timbers, in which he was severely wounded in the right elbow. Witnessing firsthand the devastation the Wyandottes suffered, he decided that the best course of action would be to support peace. He spoke passionately and forcefully to his fellow Indians during treaty negotiations with General Wayne. He was acknowledged as the leader of all the Indian nations present and was the first chief to sign the Treaty of Greenville, which established a "permanent" boundary between the Indians and the white settlers.

He died in November 1818 near "old" Upper Sandusky, now known as Cranetown. The town was later renamed in his honor. His funeral was one of the largest ever held for an Indian chief and was attended by Indians from as far away as New York, including the great orator Red Jacket. His exact burial spot was never recorded to prevent grave robbers from stealing his body.

The Tarhe Tribe No. 145 of the International Order of Red Men placed a granite marker in 1915 near Cranetown to honor the beloved chief. It was inscribed "DISTINGUISHED WYANDOT CHIEF AND LOYAL AMERICAN."

When the Ohio Territory officially became a state in 1803, the Wyandottes were living a relatively peaceful life in northern Ohio. As the War of 1812

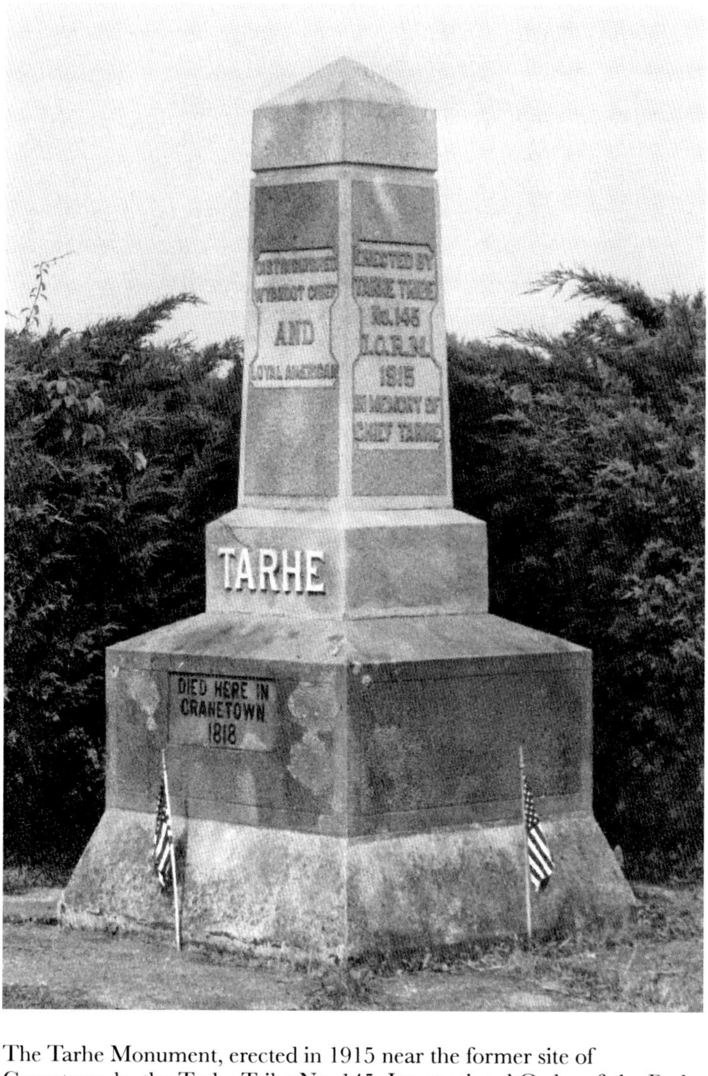

The Tarhe Monument, erected in 1915 near the former site of Cranetown by the Tarhe Tribe No. 145, International Order of the Red Men. *Wyandot County Historical Society*.

broke out, the British government tried to enlist the aid and support of the native nations in Ohio and the Michigan Territory. While a few joined the British, Chief Tarhe encouraged the Wyandottes to support the Americans, an action his nation would be rewarded for later.

During the War of 1812, it was difficult to transport troops and supplies across the Great Swamp in northwest Ohio. In order to solve this issue, military leaders decided to move supplies by river. In order to accomplish this, a series of small supply forts were constructed. One of these was Fort Ferree. Located on a bluff overlooking the Sandusky River, it was erected around the old Indian Spring, providing fresh water for the soldiers.

Lieutenant Colonel Joel Ferree, under the direction of General Richard Crooks, led soldiers of the First Regiment, Second Detachment of the Pennsylvania Militia, who were mustered into service on October 2, 1812, in Pittsburgh and served until April 15, 1813. From Pittsburgh, the soldiers marched to Upper Sandusky, where they constructed the fort in late 1812 and remained there until January 1813, when they marched north. Their service nearly complete, the soldiers headed for home on April 2, 1813.

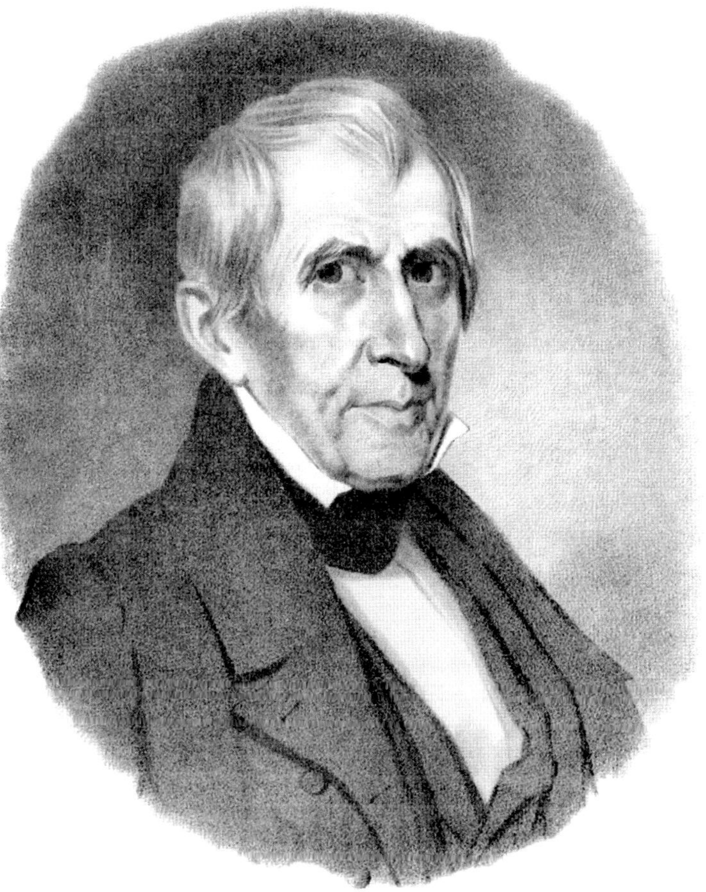

Engraving of General (later President) William Henry Harrison (1773–1841), who used Fort Ferree as his headquarters during the War of 1812. *Library of Congress.*

The fort was named in honor of Ferree, who was born on October 6, 1771, at Leacock, Pennsylvania, and died following an illness on April 9, 1813, in Zanesville, Ohio. Covering an area of roughly two acres, the wooden stockade included four blockhouses. One of these blockhouses would eventually be used as a jail on the Wyandotte Reservation. The fort was used a distribution point for food and supplies and served as the headquarters of General William Henry Harrison for a short time during the war. General Jonathan Meigs and the Ohio militia camped about a mile north of Fort Ferree on their way to Fort Meigs in August 1813. This area was known to locals as the "Grand Encampment" for many years afterward.

The Fort Ferree Graveyard was located about a quarter of a mile away on the grounds of the present Wyandot County Courthouse. During its construction in the late 1890s, remains of soldiers, along with military accoutrements from this period, were uncovered. Several soldiers were also reported as being buried beneath a large cottonwood tree, which sat in the middle of Sandusky Avenue and were discovered while removing the tree for street grading in 1875. The soldiers' remains were later reinterred in the Mission Church Cemetery.

Following the defeat of the native nations who had aligned themselves with the British during the War of 1812, the U.S. government acquired much of the land given to the Indians following the Treaty of Greenville in 1795. Treaties in 1807 and 1817 ceded nearly all of the remaining Ohio lands to the government.

3

The Wyandotte Reservations

Establishing the Reservations

Following the War of 1812 with the defeat of the British and their associated Indian nations, the balance of power shifted, with the young United States exerting more influence in the Ohio region. One of the first things the government did was to sign treaties with the established Indian nations.

On September 29, 1817, the Treaty of Maumee Rapids was signed by eight nations, including the Wyandottes, who ceded lands south of Lake Erie and along the Sandusky and St. Mary's Rivers given to them as part of the Treaty of Greenville in 1795. Article Six of the new treaty provided that in exchange, the Wyandottes would receive "a tract of land twelve miles square, at Upper Sandusky, the centre of which will be the place where fort Ferree stands, and also a tract one mile square, to be located where the chiefs direct, on a cranberry swamp, on Broken Sword creek, and to be held for the use of the tribe."

Even though the Wyandottes supported the Americans during the war, they still were forced to give up nearly 4 million acres of land in exchange for roughly 150,000 acres. This must have been a crushing blow to a proud nation. Their great leader Chief Tarhe desired peace with their neighbors, so they accepted the treaty and soon settled on their new homeland.

The Grand Reserve—or the Fort Ferree Wyandotte Reservation, as it was later referred to—was established in the western half of Crawford County in 1818. It was centered at the young village of Upper Sandusky, which grew up around the old fort.

The treaty also established several additional tracts of land to chiefs and persons abducted and eventually welcomed into the nation. One of these tracts was established along the northern edge of the primary reservation for Chief Horonu, also known as Cherokee Boy. It covered 640 acres along the Sandusky River.

Additional lands were given to the Wyandottes through the Treaty of St. Mary's on September 17, 1818. This provided for an additional sixteen-thousand-acre square tract centered at Big Spring (present-day Springville in Seneca County) along "the road leading from Upper Sandusky to Fort Findlay," including Solomon's Town and the settlements along Blanchard's Fork.

The Delaware Nation also received a tract of land in present-day Wyandot County through the Treaty of Maumee Rapids. It established a nine-mile square reservation attached to the southern edge of the Grand Reserve and included Captain Pipe's village. By this time, the town was being led by the son of Captain Pipe. His father was infamous for the torture and execution of Colonel Crawford. The Delawares resided on these lands until they ceded their reservation in 1829.

Historic Sites on the Reservations

Many remnants of the Wyandotte life on the reservation can still be seen today—the Mission Church, Walker House, Indian Mill, Nine Oaks, Stepping Stones and Indian Council House Park to name a few. Several others are known only in the historic record and include the Indian Jail, Garrett Tavern and Beery's Spring.

Nine Oaks was a clump of oak trees situated along the historic road to Carey. The area was supposedly a sacred/neutral site where chiefs of the local nations would hold councils to discuss various issues pertinent to them. One of these councils occurred in 1782, when they held the "court-martial" of Colonel William Crawford. Here the chiefs tried, convicted and sentenced Crawford to be burned at the stake to avenge the deaths of the innocent Moravian Delawares. Over the years, some of the trees have come down, making it virtually unrecognizable from its days of the Indian councils. In 1938, a cyclone came through the area and destroyed several trees, including some of these.

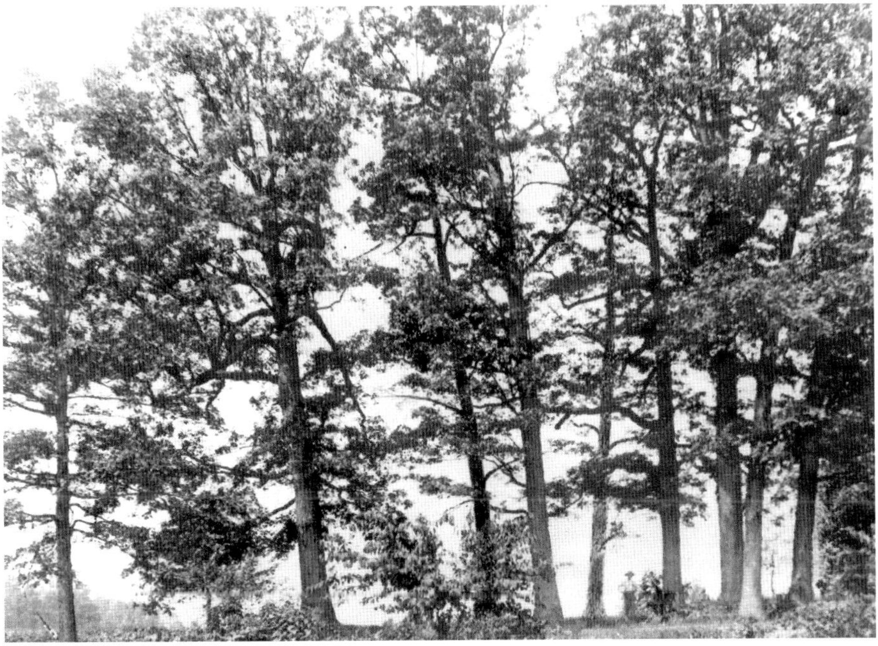

Photograph of the historic Nine Oaks, located near Carey, where Colonel William Crawford was sentenced to death in 1782 by an Indian council. *Wyandot County Historical Society.*

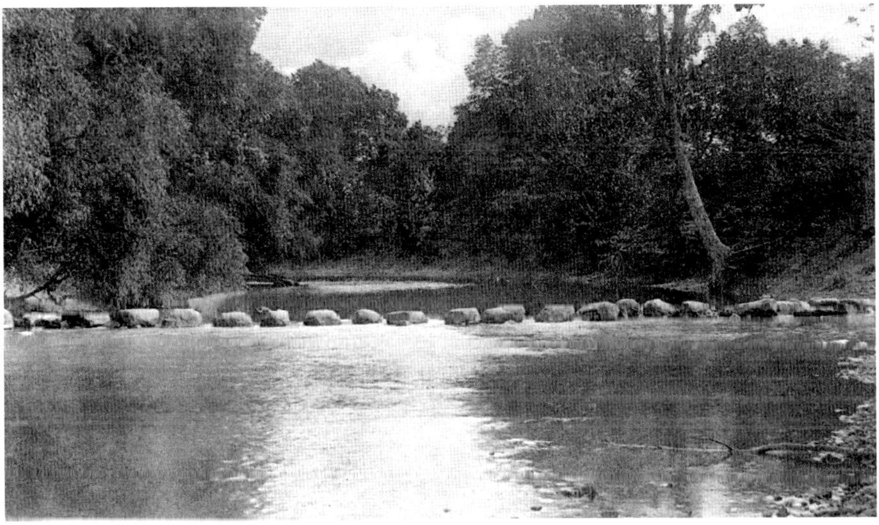

Postcard of the Stepping Stones used by the Wyandottes to cross the Sandusky River on their way to the Indian Mission Church. *Wyandot County Historical Society.*

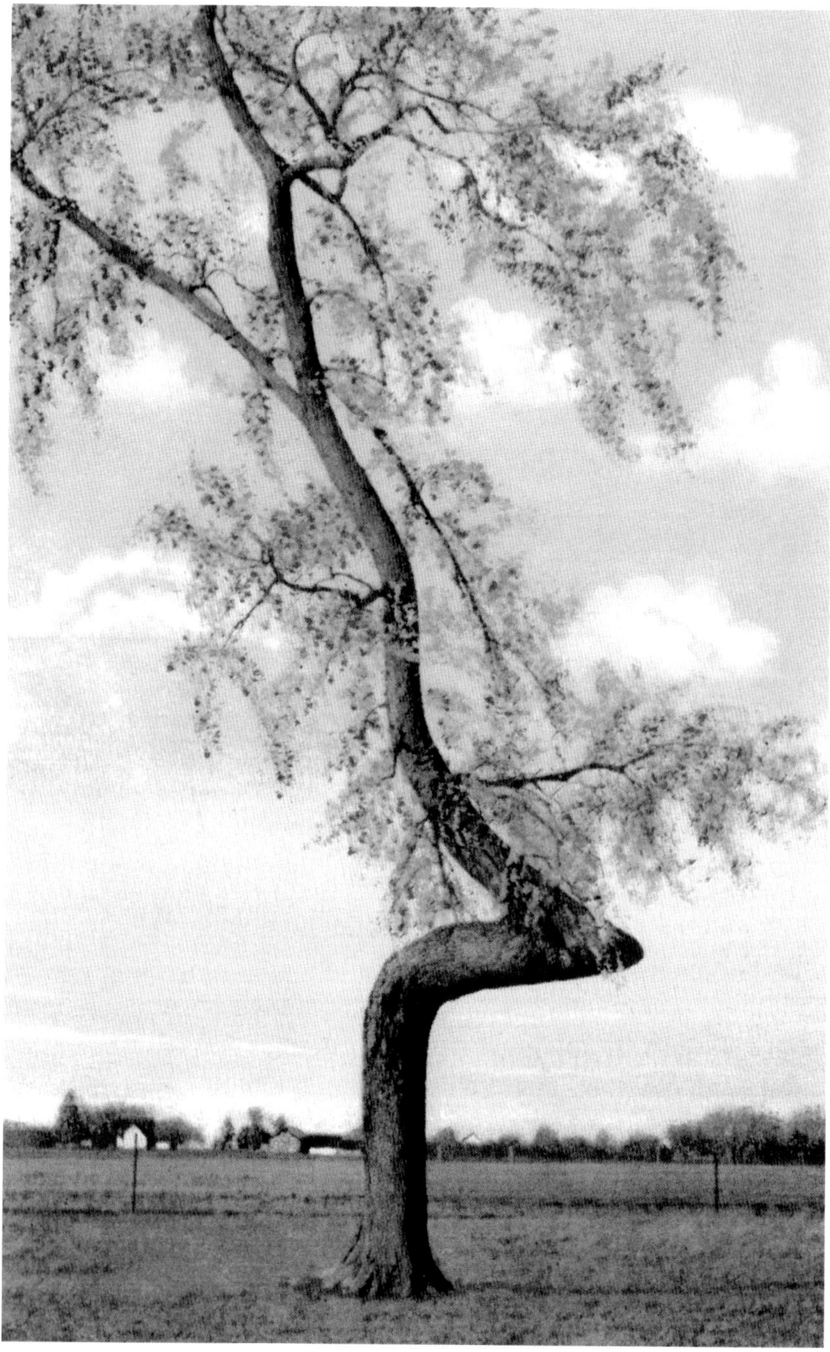

The famous Indian Trail Marker Tree, whose angled trunk reportedly pointed the way to the Grand Reserve Wyandotte Reservation. *Wyandot County Historical Society.*

To cross a low-lying section of the Sandusky River, Wyandottes reportedly placed a series of large boulders in a row, which could be walked across to stay out of the water as they walked to and from the Mission Church. Today, the area is preserved as part of Stepping Stones Park, where visitors can still walk across the stones.

Trails into and out of the Grand Reserve were marked with many landmarks. One of the best known was the Indian Trail Marker Tree, located along the west side of U.S. Route 23. Grown into the shape of a large arrow, the old elm tree supposedly pointed the way to Cranetown, the last Indian settlement in the state. According to tradition, a Wyandotte warrior bent a small sapling and tied it with grapevines so that it grew into this oddly shaped tree. It served as a guidepost along the old Indian trail until a severe storm damaged the tree beyond repair about 1967. Eventually, the county was forced to cut it down.

The Walker House, home of William Walker, a quarter-blood Wyandotte, was built about 1820 near the intersection of Walker and Fourth Streets. The house still stands as a private dwelling on Fourth Street slightly northeast of the Elks Lodge, the approximate location of Fort Ferree. Walker also erected a trading post about 1825 south of his home. By the time the pioneers began to settle in the area, the Walker Store was being operated by John Walker.

As noted earlier, the Wyandottes supported the Americans during the War of 1812 and, as a result, were rewarded for their loyalty. The Treaty of Maumee Rapids in 1817 provided that the government would "erect a saw-mill and a gristmill, upon some proper part of the Wyandot reservation, for their use." The spot chosen was along the west bank of the Sandusky River about three miles north of Upper Sandusky. Charles Garrett was selected to construct the mills.

Construction on the mill dam and sawmill was begun in 1819. The sawmill reportedly used an "up and down saw." By the next year, the two mills had been completed. It is believed this was the first and only time the government built multiple mills on an Indian reservation with federal funds. It is unknown exactly how the original mills appeared, as no images survive and only brief descriptions of the buildings exist. It is known that the gristmill was a single-story, square building constructed of walnut. According to Indian agent Colonel John Johnston's notes, the mills and dam cost about $4,000 to erect. According to Harry Kinley's notes, John Garrett built the mills.

The U.S. government appointed millers to operate the mills for the Wyandottes, and Charles White was reportedly the first one appointed. He earned fifteen dollars a month during his three years. On May 2, 1825, a group of Wyandotte chiefs, including Warpole, Mononcue and Between-the-Logs, met at the council house to draft a resolution regarding the operation of the Indian Mill. The resolution allowed Reverend James Finley to sign a contract with "some competent person to attend the Indian Mill, provided the wages shall not exceed $375 per year." This contract was signed with Charles Garrett, who worked there for two years. He was followed as miller by Jonathan Briley, John Johnson and Lewis Rummel.

About 1835, a fire destroyed the original one-story gristmill. Needing funds to rebuild the mill, as well as pay other expenses, a five-mile-wide strip of land off the east end of the reservation was sold at a public auction in Marion, Ohio. The new mill was erected in 1836 and served the Wyandottes until they left for Kansas in 1843. The mills were leased to various millers until being purchased at public auction by George Myers in 1848. The sawmill and gristmill were dismantled in 1861 with the salvaged materials used by millwright Lewis Rummel to erect the current Indian Mill.

The Wyandotte Council House was located at Cranetown (then known as Upper Sandusky) until Chief Tarhe's death in 1818. This building stood

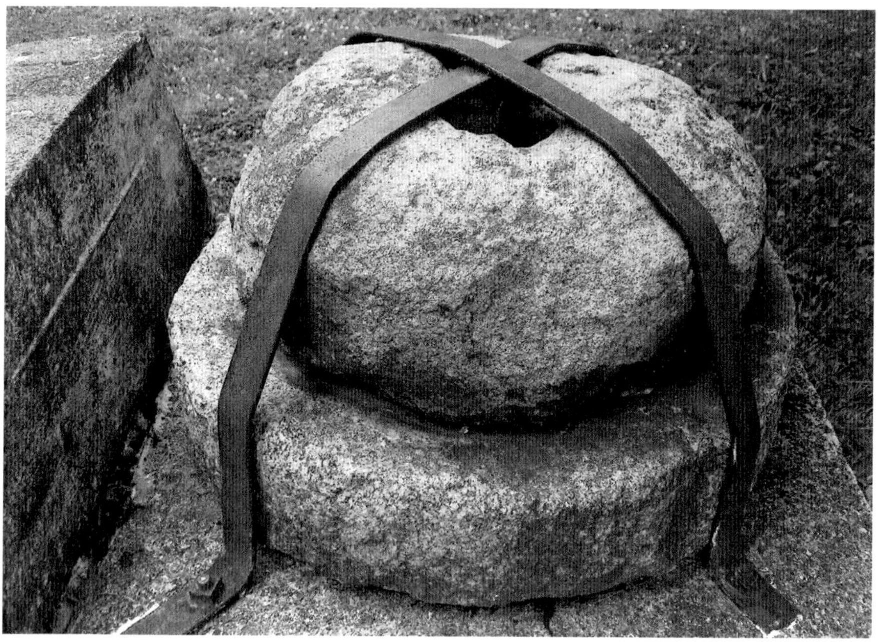

Grinding stones used by the Wyandotte Indians to process grain prior to the erection of the original Indian Mill in 1820. *Author's collection.*

approximately a mile and a half north of the village. It was constructed primarily of split logs set between uprights with tree bark covering the roof and a dirt floor. The structure measured roughly one hundred feet long by fifteen feet wide. Logs were placed on their sides for seats. Shortly after Tarhe's death, the Council House was moved to present-day Upper Sandusky. The former village was renamed Cranetown in honor of Chief Tarhe.

The new Council House was constructed similarly to the earlier structure on a bluff overlooking the west end of today's Harrison Smith Park. It was replaced in 1830 by a small, two-story frame structure (eighteen by twenty-four feet) that resembled the other log structures in the area. The logs were prepared at the Wyandotte sawmill, located north of the village. It was used until the Wyandottes left in 1843.

Moses H. Kirby later acquired the old Council House and land. According to Wyandot County commissioners' records, on April 16, 1845, the commissioners authorized the county auditor "to issue an order in favor of Col. Kirby for $30 in full payment of his interest in said house." The old structure was soon repaired and furnished "for the accommodation of the county officers." The old Council House witnessed the first session of the Court of Common Pleas of Wyandot County on July 1, 1845. Realizing the limitations of the "courthouse," the commissioners began the process to replace the old structure in January 1846. Sold for $250 to a local businessman in 1850, the building was used as a print shop and eventually a schoolhouse. A fire consumed the wood structure and all its contents in 1851, ending the story of one of Upper Sandusky's more prominent buildings.

The location of the Wyandotte Council House and a nearby cemetery are commemorated in a small park overlooking the bluff. Recently, excavations uncovered several limestone foundation stones from the structure. Two of these stone fragments were presented to the Wyandot County Museum for display.

Hearing a calling to preach to the Wyandottes, John Stewart arrived in Upper Sandusky in 1816. His missionary work started out slow; however, he was able to convert several of the chiefs. As his mission grew, it caught the attention of the Methodist Church and, in 1819, became the first officially recognized mission of the Methodist Episcopal Church in the United States. Stewart was followed by Reverend John Wheeler and Reverend James B. Finley. Soon a log school and one-mile square farm were added to the mission.

The Mission Farm was located on a bluff overlooking the Sandusky River about 825 feet northeast of the burial grounds near the Wyandotte Council House. Seven chiefs signed a petition in August 1821 requesting the organization of a school to accompany the mission in Upper Sandusky.

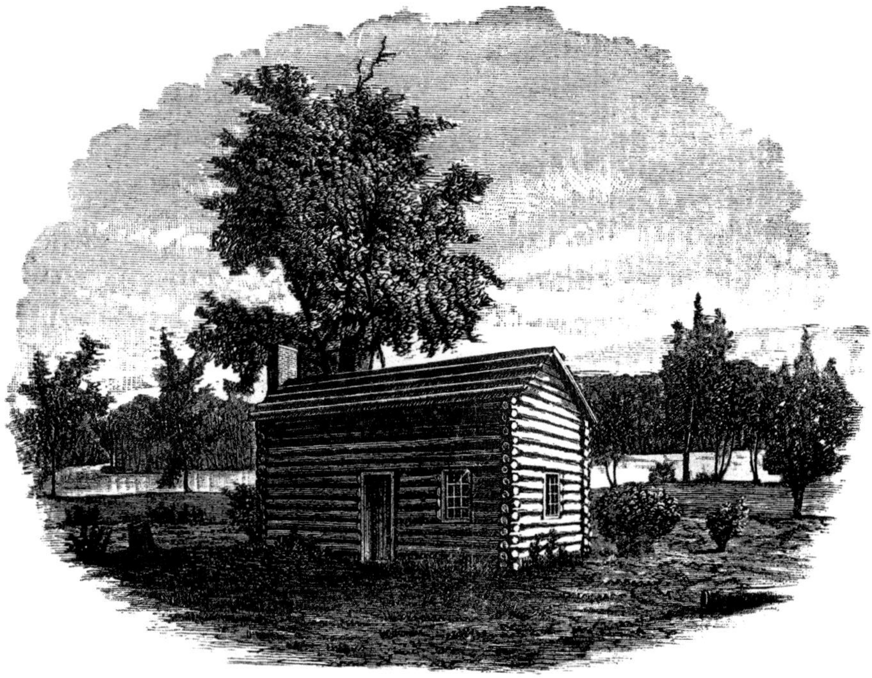

Sketch of the Wyandotte Mission School by Henry Howe in 1846. This was the first integrated, coeducational industrial school in America. *From* Historical Collections of Ohio, *1891.*

Reverend Finley was sent to assist Stewart in the creation of a "manual training school." A hewn-log school structure with planks and joists sawed at the new Wyandotte sawmill was erected along the Sandusky River about a half mile north of Upper Sandusky, and the school opened on October 16, 1821. Fifty-one children were listed on a school roster dated August 23, 1823.

In the new Mission School, the girls were taught domestic skills, such as cooking, baking and sewing, while the boys were taught manual trades—farming, blacksmithing and woodworking. Thus began the first coeducational industrial school in America. Another unique aspect of the school was that it accepted Indian, white and black children and educated them together, creating perhaps the first integrated, multicultural school in the young country.

Mother Solomon was born Margaret Grey Eyes on November 29, 1816, somewhere near Owl Creek in Marion County. Her father was John "Squire" Grey Eyes, who gave the passionate "Farewell Address" upon the Wyandottes' removal in 1843. When the Mission School opened in 1821, she was the first young Wyandotte girl taken to be taught there. As she grew up, she continued to attend the school and attended services at the Mission Church, becoming acquainted with all the missionaries.

When she was just seventeen, she married David Young on February 4, 1833. The couple would have eight children. Unfortunately, all of them died young. When the Wyandottes moved west, David and Margaret took their young family with them. In Kansas, David worked as a ferryman until his death in 1852. He is buried near two of their children in Huron Cemetery in Kansas City, Kansas.

Six years later, Margaret married John Solomon, who was the sheriff of the Wyandotte Territory. Eventually, she became homesick for where she grew up in Ohio, so Margaret convinced John and a nephew, Jimmy Guyami, to return to Ohio. In 1865, the group moved back to the former reservation, reportedly settling in a small cabin she had inhabited prior to leaving Ohio. John, by this time working as a tailor, died in 1876. Sixty years old, she never remarried and instead found joy in being a surrogate mom and community babysitter. Hence, she received the nickname "Mother" Solomon. Many older residents would happily proclaim that they were raised by her.

In 1889, when the Central Ohio Conference of the Methodist Episcopal Church dedicated the restored Wyandotte Mission Church, Mother Solomon was the only Wyandotte present who had attended services in the original building. She played a small role in the ceremony by singing in her native language the hymn "Come Thou Fount of Every Blessing," which she had learned there. Following her part, a small collection worth twenty-five dollars was taken up on her behalf.

Toward late July 1890, she was getting weaker and, sensing the end was near, allowed herself to be removed to the home of Mr. and Mrs. Jacob Hayman. She passed away on August 18, 1890, the last full-blooded Wyandotte from the Grand Reserve to live in what is present-day Wyandot County. Two days later, Mother Solomon's funeral service was held in her beloved Mission Church. Despite a heavy rain, a huge crowd turned out to watch her funeral. She was buried in the church cemetery near the graves of her fellow Wyandottes in a fenced plot behind the church beside her second husband.

The missionaries and Wyandottes both felt the need for a permanent church structure in which to hold their services. A group led by Reverend Finley traveled to Washington, D.C., in 1823 to request funds owed the Wyandotte Nation. After speaking with representatives of President James Monroe, the delegation received $1,333 in government bonds from Secretary

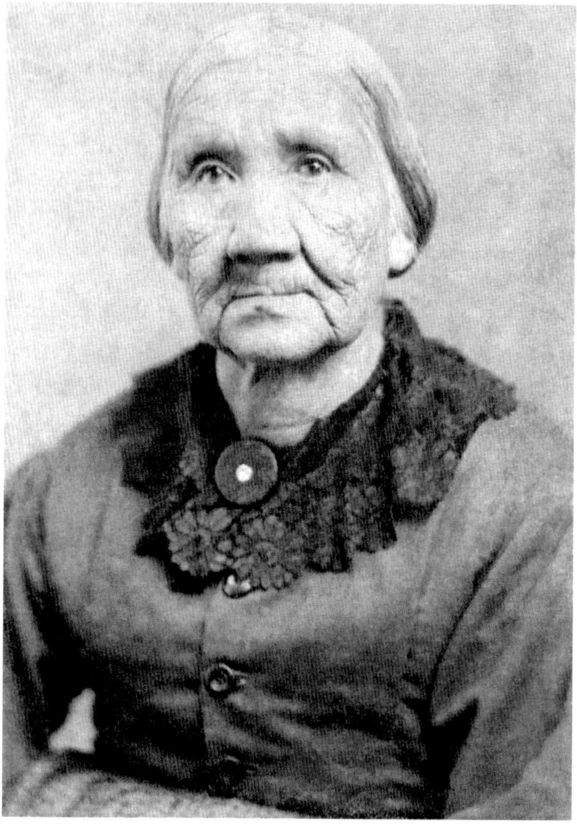

Left: Mother Solomon (1816–1890), born Margaret Grey Eyes, was the last original Wyandotte from the Grand Reserve to live in present-day Wyandot County. *Wyandot County Historical Society*.

Below: West and south views of the Indian Mission Church, which was originally built in 1824 and restored in 1889. *Wyandot County Historical Society*.

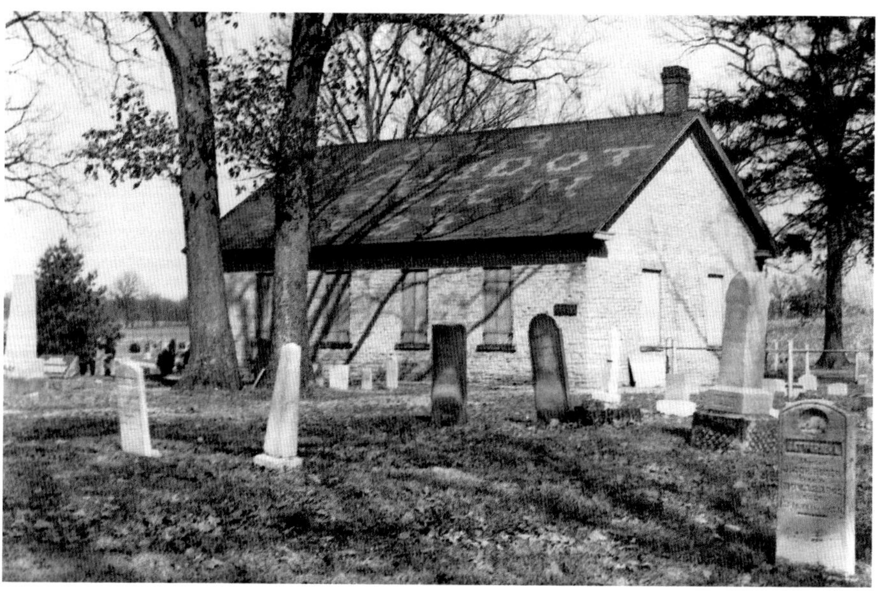

of War John C. Calhoun to use toward the construction of the church. This is believed to have been the first time government funds were used to erect a church on reservation lands.

A secluded spot surrounded by trees was selected north of town. Reverend Finley oversaw construction of the new Mission Church. The one-room structure, situated inside a small enclosure, was constructed of Sandusky River blue limestone, local logs prepared at the Wyandotte sawmill and slate for the roof. Measuring thirty by forty feet, the new church was completed in 1824. The Wyandottes faithfully worshiped at the church every Sunday until they left for Kansas in July 1843.

In order to ensure that their beloved church and the graves of their ancestors were protected, tribal leaders deeded one acre containing the burial grounds, plus two acres surrounding and containing the Mission Church, to the Methodist Episcopal Church, which agreed to preserve and protect these lands. An interesting note is that since the acreage for the church was given directly from the Wyandottes out of reservation lands, it has never been formally owned by the U.S. government.

For a period, the Methodist Episcopal Church leaders made good on their promise of keeping up the church and graveyard. Eventually, the old burial grounds on the bluff were entirely neglected. Many of the old grave stones were broken or removed entirely until only a handful remained. Without the markers, the graves were nearly indistinguishable from the surrounding grounds. The Mission Church sat on the northern edge of town and was sparingly used for services, primarily by new denominations looking for a temporary house of worship.

The Mission Church soon found itself neglected and slowly sank into a deplorable condition. By the 1870s, the walls and roof had begun to collapse. The stone markers surrounding it were covered in overgrowth, and the elements made several of the stones illegible. In the mid-1880s, an itinerant Methodist preacher by the name of Reverend Nathaniel Barrett Coulson Love traveled to Upper Sandusky and was heartbroken to see the condition of the old church. Along with a group of local businessmen, he attempted to convince the Methodist Episcopal Church to repair the old church. Determined to make amends, in 1888, the General Conference of the Methodist Episcopal Church appropriated $2,000 to restore the Mission Church. Work was begun in 1889 and completed a few months later. Using stone from the same quarry and local woods, the building was restored as nearly as possible to its original appearance.

The restored Mission Church was dedicated with impressive ceremonies in front of a large crowd on September 21, 1889. The General Conference of the Methodist Church designated the Mission Church a National United Methodist Historic Shrine in 1960. It is one of twelve recognized Methodist Shrines in the United States. The Mission Church was listed on the National Register of Historic Places on January 20, 1976. Currently operated by the John Stewart United Methodist Church, it offers tours and nondenominational services during the summer months.

John Stewart was born about 1786 in Powhatten County, Virginia. Despite their mixed blood (black, white and Native American), his parents were free citizens and practiced the Baptist religion. He was raised in Virginia and Tennessee. As an adult, he traveled to Ohio, where he was robbed. Feeling depressed, he tried to drink himself to death until he came upon a Methodist camp meeting. Requested to speak at the gathering, he initially resisted but soon felt the call to preach. Sometime afterward, he reportedly heard the voice of a man and woman telling him to minister to the natives.

Setting off in a northwesterly direction, he came across the Delaware Nation, where he preached and sang. Soon he was headed off toward the Wyandottes, who reportedly had never heard the words of the Bible. Stewart did not speak the language of the Wyandottes, so he approached and soon befriended Indian sub-agent William Walker, who introduced him to Jonathan Pointer. A black man who had been kidnapped as a youth and later adopted into the Wyandottes, Pointer knew the language but had an immediate distrust of Stewart. A nonbeliever, Pointer agreed to translate Stewart's words but, according to Stewart's biography, always added a disparaging remark afterward like, "That's what the preacher says, but I don't believe it."

Stewart's first sermon was delivered under a tree to a single Wyandotte in 1816 near the village of Cranetown. His singing voice soon attracted additional Wyandottes who came more for his melodic voice than his words. Following the conversion of Between-the-Logs, additional chiefs and women listened to his words and converted as well. As an unlicensed missionary who felt the call, he was accused by other pastors of preaching without a license. Three years after starting his work, Stewart approached the Methodist Episcopal Church, which licensed him and formally recognized the Wyandotte Mission. In 1820, primarily due to Stewart's work, the Methodist Missionary Society was formed.

Ill health soon forced Stewart to retire to a small farm outside Upper Sandusky. Reverend James B. Finley was appointed in 1821 by the Methodist

Episcopal Church to continue the mission. In 1823, one year before the Indian Mission Church was erected, Stewart died and was buried on his small farm. When the Wyandottes left for Kansas in 1843 his body was reinterred in the Mission Church graveyard to protect it. On the 100th anniversary of his arrival, a large boulder with a bronze plaque was placed in a small enclosure behind the church. It was inscribed with Stewart's last words to his beloved Wyandottes: "Be Faithful."

Between-the-Logs supported the Americans just as Chief Tarhe had. He was born about 1780 near Lower Sandusky to a Seneca father and a Wyandotte mother of the Bear Clan. He participated in the ill-fated campaign against General "Mad Anthony" Wayne and was a trusted confident of the head chief, who sent him on various missions for the nation. During two of

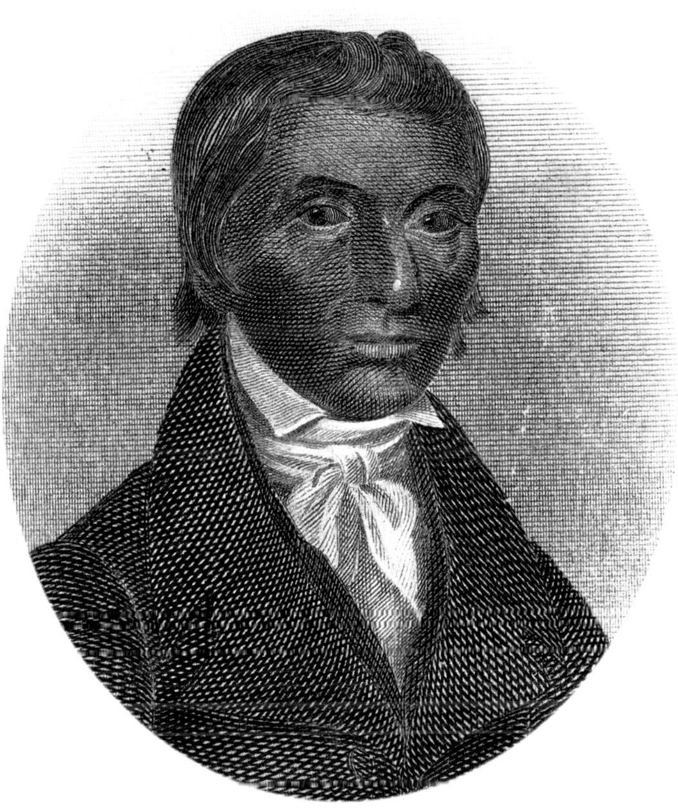

Cabinet card image of Wyandotte chief Between-the-Logs (1780–1827), Reverend John Stewart's first convert, based on an engraving by T.D. Booth. *Wyandot County Historical Society.*

these, he uncovered the fallacies of a celebrated Seneca prophet and Tenskwatawa, a renowned Shawnee prophet and the brother of Tecumseh. Protecting the Wyandotte Nation from further losses, his efforts led him to quickly rise to the rank of chief.

He was considered the chief speaker of the Wyandottes due to his great memory and high ability in discussions. During the Indian council at Brownstown, Michigan, he was the head chief of the Wyandottes and rejected all efforts to join the British against the Americans during the War of 1812. The Wyandottes soon left the council and joined the Americans, even accompanying General William Henry Harrison as he invaded Canada. Following the war, Between-the-Logs settled near Upper Sandusky and eventually became John Stewart's first convert during his struggling missionary work. Between-the-Logs died in 1827 following an illness and was buried in Mission Church Cemetery.

The Indian Jail on the reservation was originally one of Fort Ferree's four blockhouses, erected in 1812. When the Grand Reserve was established in 1817, the structure was moved to serve as a jail for the Wyandottes. It sat near the south end of Third Street.

The two-story structure was constructed of hewed logs about eight to ten inches thick. It measured roughly eighteen by fourteen feet and was situated north–south with a view of the "Sandusky Bottoms" to the south and east. Each floor was about eight feet high and consisted of one room with a window on the south side and a single entrance with two doors on the north. There was a heavy batten outer door and an iron-grated inner door. The roof projected over the north side about eight feet, providing some protection from the elements. The second floor was accessed via an exterior stairwell that began in the northwest corner.

The structure suited the needs of the reservation, but the new Wyandot County commissioners soon decided to erect a new jail. A contract for a new two-story brick jail was awarded in October 1845 in the amount of $3,240. John Key's brickyard provided the bricks for the construction. By 1849, the jail had been completed, and about a year later, the old Indian Jail was torn down.

The Garrett Tavern, erected about 1817 by William Walker Jr. and his brother-in-law George Garrett, was a two-story double-log structure measuring roughly eighteen by thirty feet. It once stood near the intersection of Wyandot Avenue and Fourth Street along the Harrison Road. William Walker Jr.'s youngest sister, Maria, was married to George Garrett. The old Overland Stagecoach stop was the only inn located in Upper Sandusky during the time

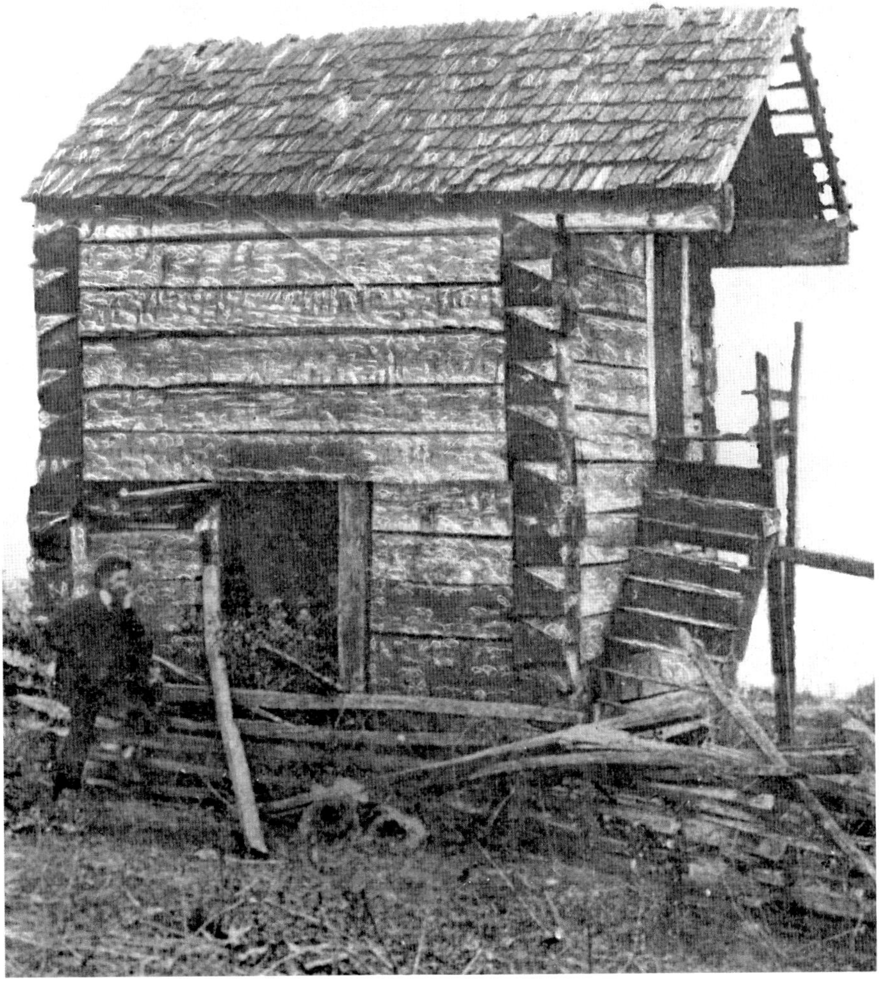

The Indian Jail on the Grand Reserve was originally a blockhouse associated with Fort Ferree and overlooked the Sandusky River. *Wyandot County Historical Society.*

of the Wyandottes. It is perhaps best known as the location where the famous British writer Charles Dickens spent the night on April 21, 1842.

From January to June 1842, Charles Dickens traveled across North America and recounted his adventures in a travelogue published as *American Notes for General Circulation* in 1842. He spent the night in Upper Sandusky at Garrett Tavern across from the famous Beery's Spring and unflatteringly recounted his somewhat unpleasant night in this book.

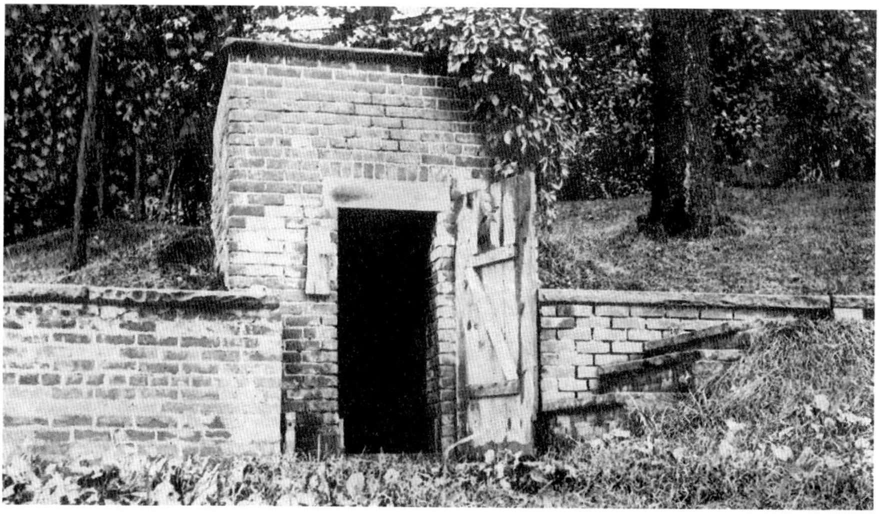

Brick structure used to protect Beery's Spring in the early 1900s. The spring provided fresh water to natives, soldiers and pioneers. *Wyandot County Historical Society.*

Beery's Spring was a natural spring used by local Indians, including the Wyandottes, from the early 1700s until 1843. Colonel Crawford's men drank from the spring on June 4, 1782, en route to the Battle of Sandusky Plains. It also served as a source of fresh, clean drinking water for Lieutenant Colonel Joel Ferree's troops, who built their fort surrounding it. Many other soldiers and travelers drank from the spring as they passed through the area. One of the best known was Charles Dickens, who drank from the spring during his stay at the Garrett Tavern in 1842.

Originally known as the Old Indian Spring, it received its new name from the Beery family, who, at one time, owned the land it was located on. The spring was located near the Garrett Tavern on the north side of Kirby Hill overlooking the Sandusky River near the current site of the Elks Lodge on East Wyandot Avenue. Surrounded by large trees and bushes, these were eventually removed and a small brick structure erected to protect the spring. One of the large trees protecting the spring was cut down on January 13, 1888. Charles Shealy recovered the tree and created several pieces of furniture from it. Unfortunately, Beery's Spring was lost during water and sewer pipe upgrades during the 1960s.

Ceding the Reservations

The U.S. government passed the Indian Removal Act in 1830. It was designed to relocate all of the Indian nations east of the Mississippi River to the West. The goal was to remove all the Indians peacefully to new reservations; however, force could be used if necessary to make the nations comply. It also gave President Andrew Jackson complete control over all the natives in America. Treaties were signed fairly quickly with many of the larger or troublesome nations. Due to its peaceful nature and small size, the Wyandotte Nation was ignored at the time.

Late in 1831, the Wyandottes residing on the Big Spring Reservation began to be concerned with the large influx of white settlers surrounding them. On January 19, 1832, they signed the Treaty of McCutcheonville, Ohio, in which they agreed to cede the entire sixteen-acre reservation granted to them in 1817 back to the federal government. It began by recording that the Wyandottes were "fully convinced that, whilst they remain in their present situation in the State of Ohio, in the vicinity of a white population, which is continually increasing and crowding around them, they cannot prosper and be happy, and the morals of many of their people will be daily becoming more and more vitiated." In exchange for their lands, the nation was offered land west of the Mississippi River. Instead of accepting the offer, it refused the lands and retained the right to return to Canada or to the reservation along the Huron River in Michigan maintained by its fellow Wyandottes.

Tensions between the nation and white settlers surrounding the Fort Ferree Reservation continued to grow until 1842, when the Wyandottes agreed to cede their lands and head west. Although it was not what they desired, it was ultimately decided that this was best for the tribal members. On March 17, 1842, the Treaty with the Wyandottes (also known as the Treaty of Upper Sandusky) was signed, and the Wyandottes ceded to the U.S. government "all that tract of land situate, lying, and being in the county of Crawford and State of Ohio, commonly known as the residue of the large reserve." Article 1 further ceded "all their right and title to the Wyandotte Reserve, on both sides of the river Huron, in the State of Michigan." In exchange, the government agreed to provide a tract of land west of the Mississippi River containing 148,000 acres for the Wyandotte Nation.

Members of the Michigan reservation and several Wyandottes from Canada traveled to Upper Sandusky in March prior to the exodus to Kansas. Before their departure, Squire Grey Eyes gave a passionate speech that came to be known as the "Farewell Address." On July 12, 1843, 664

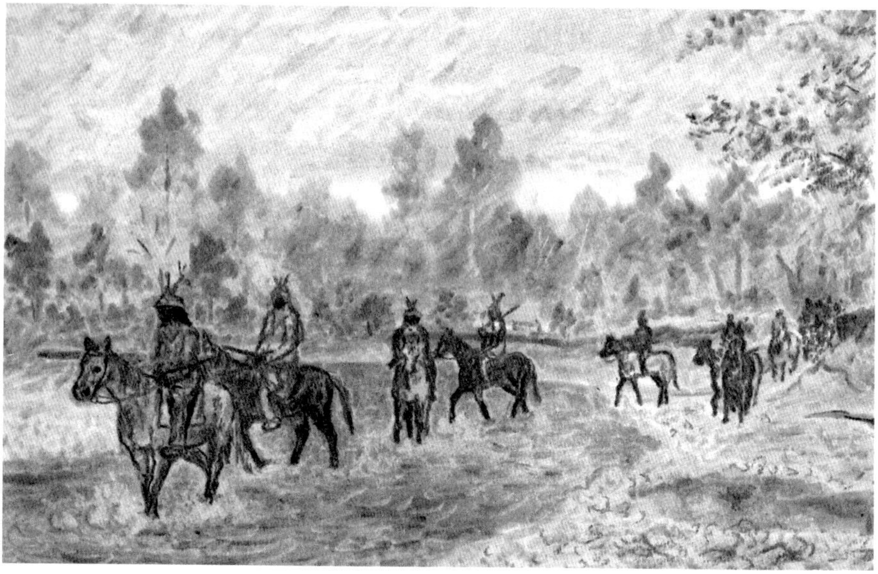

Portion of a charcoal sketch, completed by local artist Frank Halbedel in 1888, depicting the Wyandotte Exodus from Ohio in 1843. *Wyandot County Historical Society.*

Wyandottes, including 25 from Michigan and 30 from Canada, headed south. They traveled by foot, on horseback and in 120 wagons and buggies toward Cincinnati, arriving on July 19.

Two days later, the group boarded the steamships *Republic* and *Nodaway*. Following the Ohio and Mississippi Rivers, the ships landed at St. Louis on July 24. Four days later, the *Republic* reached the town of Kansas (present-day Kansas City, Missouri), and the *Nodaway* arrived on the thirty-first. The western lands promised to them never materialized, so the Wyandottes were forced to purchase land in Kansas from the Delaware Nation. The government compensated the Wyandotte Nation for the promised acreage and paid off the debt owed to the Delaware Nation in 1850. Thus began the next chapter in the long story of the Wyandotte Nation.

Establishing a New County

In order to understand how Wyandot County came into being, one must first examine the history of Crawford County, from which much of Wyandot was derived. In 1787, Reverend Manasseh Cutler wrote the Northwest Ordinance of 1787, which governed the lands of the Northwest Territory. One year prior to Ohio's establishment in 1803, the Ohio Constitution divided its portion of the Northwest Territory into three districts, with Crawford County located in District Two.

Maxwell Ludlow began to survey the lands that would later become Crawford and Wyandot Counties in 1807. He completed the surveys of Polk, Jackson, Vernon and Auburn Townships. Deputy Surveyor General Silvanus Bourne completed the survey of the remaining townships in 1819.

The General Assembly of the state of Ohio passed an act on February 12, 1820, creating several counties in northwestern Ohio out of the lands ceded by the Indians to the federal government. These lands, referred to at the time as the New Purchase, were bounded to the north by Lake Erie and Michigan; to the east by a line drawn from Lake Erie to Cardington, Morrow County; to the south by a line drawn from Cardington to Indiana; and to the west by Indiana.

Named for Colonel William Crawford, this was the seventh county created from these lands. Along with Marion County, it was attached to Delaware County, where many of the early records are held. In 1824, the judicial "county seat" was relocated to Marion County. It was not until April 1, 1827, that Crawford County was organized and established as its own

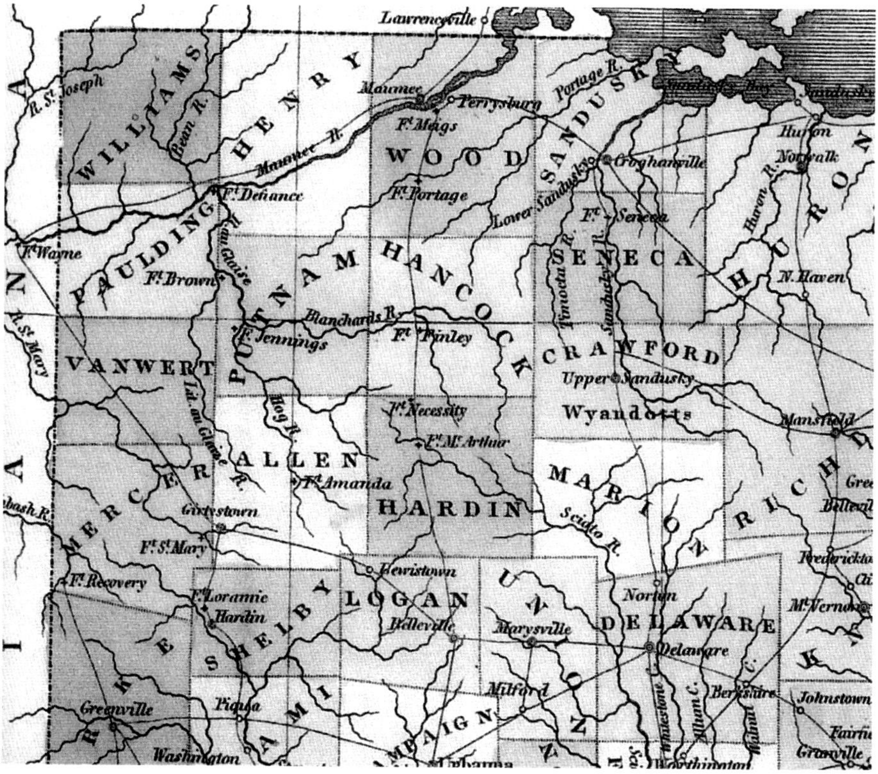

Northwest Ohio portion of an 1828 map by Anthony Finley showing Upper Sandusky and "Wyandotts" in Crawford County. *From* General Atlas, *1828.*

distinct entity. The new Wyandotte reservations that had been established by the Treaty of Maumee Rapids in 1817 were located in the western half of Crawford County.

Following the removal of the Wyandotte Indians to Kansas in 1843, the Ohio government decided to create Wyandot County by utilizing the former reservation and additional lands from western Crawford County, southeast Hancock County, northwest Marion County and northeast Hardin County. On February 3, 1845, the Ohio legislature passed a statute entitled "An Act to Erect the New County of Wyandott, and Alter the Boundaries of the County of Crawford." This legislation outlined the portions of the surrounding counties to be removed and attached to the former reservation creating Wyandot County proper, which covers approximately 408 square miles. The county is the eighty-eighth alphabetically but was the eighty-fourth to be organized in Ohio.

The new county was divided into thirteen townships in 1845. Only Crane Township was comprised entirely of former reservation lands. Salem and Mifflin Townships were created out of reservation lands and part of Crawford County. Sycamore and Crawford Townships were created out of reservation lands and part of Crawford County's Crawford Township (1825). Tymochtee Township was created out of reservation lands and part of Crawford County's Tymochtee Township (1825). Eden Township was created out of reservation lands and part of Crawford County's Leith Township (1838). Jackson Township was created from part of Hardin County's Jackson Township (1836) and Goshen Township (1834). Ridge Township was part of Hancock County's Amanda Township (1828) while Richland was part of Hancock County's Delaware Township (1829). Pitt Township was created from reservation lands and part of Marion County's Salt Rock Township (1824). Marseilles Township was created from Hardin County's Goshen Township (1834) and Marion County's Grand Township (1824). Antrim Township was created from reservation lands, part of Crawford County's Bucyrus Township (1820) and Marion County's Grand Prairie Township (1824). Local lawyer John Sears was credited at the time with selecting the formal spelling of Wyandot, which was chosen from three different versions.

Upper Sandusky was established on March 3, 1843, by order of the U.S. government and surveyed by Lewis Clawson in November and December 1843. Its settlement was sparse until the spring of 1845. The town was named for its location near the headwaters of the Sandusky River, which flows north to Lake Erie. The word Sandusky is an Anglicized version of the Indian word *sa-un-dus-tee*, which reportedly means "water within pools" in the Wyandotte language. Through conversations with the state, Upper Sandusky was selected as the county seat at the time of the county's establishment.

Wyandot County commissioners Stephen Fowler, William Griffith and Ethan Terry authorized the selling of town lots in the new village of Upper Sandusky beginning on August 20, 1845. Every third town lot would be sold up to a maximum of 121 In-Lots and 72 Out-Lots. In October 1845, the sale of additional lots was commenced. The first frame structure erected in the city was built in 1846 by David and William Ayers. The town was officially incorporated on February 18, 1848, by an act of the Ohio General Assembly.

Once the new county was established, public buildings were needed to conduct the county's business. The first courthouse in the county was not an imposing brick or stone structure, nor was it even erected by residents of the new county. It was actually the old Wyandotte Council House, erected

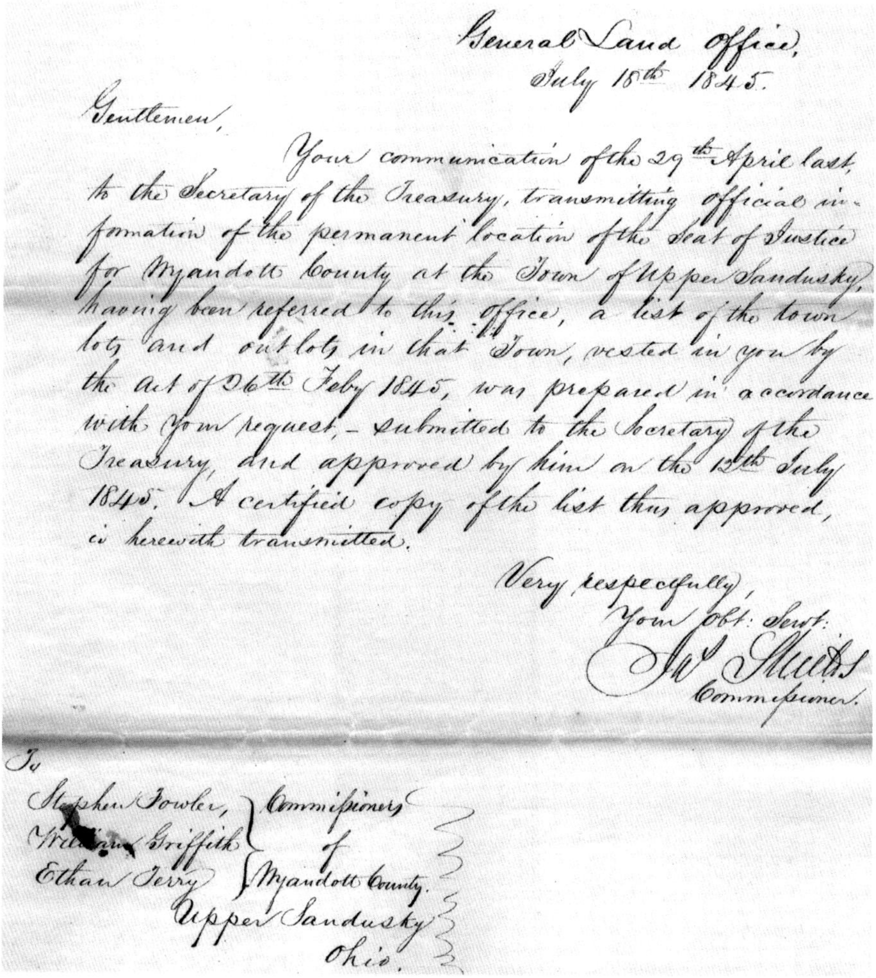

General Land Office,
July 18th 1845.

Gentlemen,

Your communication of the 29th April last, to the Secretary of the Treasury, transmitting official information of the permanent location of the Seat of Justice for Wyandott County at the Town of Upper Sandusky, having been referred to this office, a list of the town lots and outlots in that Town, vested in you by the Act of 26th Feby 1845, was prepared in accordance with your request, - submitted to the Secretary of the Treasury, and approved by him on the 12th July 1845. A certified copy of the list thus approved, is herewith transmitted.

Very respectfully,
Your obt: Servt:
Jas Shields
Commissioner.

To
Stephen Fowler, William Griffith, Ethan Terry } Commissioners of Wyandott County.
Upper Sandusky
Ohio.

Letter dated July 18, 1845, to the Wyandot County commissioners from the General Land Office referring to Upper Sandusky as the permanent county seat. *Wyandot County Historical Society*.

about 1830 on the Grand Reserve. The building stood on a lot near the old Wyandotte burial grounds on the bluff overlooking present-day Harrison Smith Park. A handful of gravestones survive to mark the location today, which was originally surrounded by a crude wooden fence. In 2014, work near the site uncovered original limestone blocks that had been used as foundation stones for the building

Due to the limitations of this building, officials recognized the need for a larger, more permanent stone courthouse for the county. On October 2, 1845,

Public Sale OF TOWN LOTS at UPPER SANDUSKY.

THE Commissioners of Wyandot County, will offer the following valuable Town Property for sale at UPPER SANDUSKY, Ohio, upon the 20th, 21st & 22d days of AUGUST next, to wit: The In and Out Lots in the town of Upper Sandusky, vested in the said Commissioners by act of Congress, approved February 26, 1845, being every third of the In and Out Lots selected by alternate aud progressive numbers, amounting to One Hundred and Twenty-six In-lots and Seventy-two Out-lots.

Upper Sandusky, a town laid out by the General Government, is delightfully situated on the Sandusky river, near the centre of the WYANDOT RESERVE, and the seat of Justice of the new County of Wyandot has been permanently fixed at said Town.

TERMS OF SALE.--One-fourth of the purchase Money required in hand, the balance in three annual instalments secured by notes bearing interest.

STEPHEN FOWLER,
WILLIAM GRIFFITH,
ETHAN TERRY.

ATTEST: SAMUEL M. WORTH, Auditor.
August 2, 1845.

Official newspaper notice from the Wyandot County commissioners dated August 2, 1845, announcing the terms for the sale of town lots in Upper Sandusky. *From* Wyandott Telegraph, *August 9, 1845.*

it was ordered by the Wyandot County commissioners "that four hundred and ten dollars be appropriated out of the moneys received from the sale of lots to pay for In-Lots numbered 145 and 146," which, in addition to In-Lot number 147, were set aside and designated as the site for the new county courthouse and jail. Moneys from the sale of every third lot would be placed into a special fund for the purpose of erecting Wyandot County's new public structures. By June 11, 1853, the officials of the county had received $15,224.24 in cash from the government of the United States, which was an amount sufficient to purchase the lots and to construct the courthouse and jail buildings.

On June 4, 1846, the county commissioners authorized a newspaper advertisement calling for design specifications for a new courthouse. In September 1846, the commissioners entered into a contract with William Young to erect the courthouse for $7,000. Young had the contract reassigned to John W. Kennedy and John H. Junkins. By the spring of 1849, the structure still was not finished, so the commissioners signed a third agreement with John H. Junkins to erect the structure for $9,800. The building was finally completed near the end of 1849 and fully occupied in 1850, at which time the commissioners sold the old Wyandotte Council House. In October 1851,

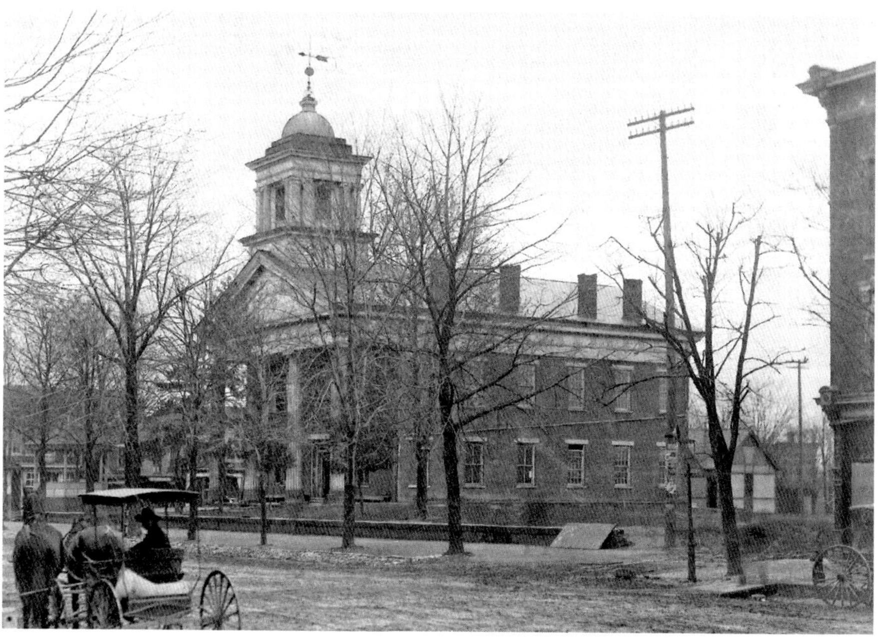

View of the southwest corner of the "Greek temple–style" Wyandot County Courthouse, which was erected in 1849 and stood until 1897. *Wyandot County Historical Society.*

Junkins was authorized an additional $2,200 for his work, bringing the total cost for the second Wyandot County Courthouse to $12,000.

Many small towns sprang up throughout the county in the mid- to late 1800s. Most have disappeared or are little more than a crossroads on the map today. Several cities, such as Carey, Sycamore, Marseilles, Harpster and Nevada, have grown and prospered since they were platted.

Carey was laid out in 1843 by R.M. Shuler and W.J. Buell on land that they owned. It was surveyed by Judge Beidler, chief engineer of the Mad River Railroad, and named in honor of Judge John Carey, who was elected to the Ohio House of Representatives in 1828, 1836 and 1843 and served in the U.S. House of Representatives from 1859 to 1861. The first town lots were sold in 1847. On June 2, 1858, the small village was finally incorporated.

Sycamore was surveyed in 1842 and was named for the numerous sycamore trees lining Sycamore Creek. The first house erected in what became the town was a log structure erected in 1836 by George Harper, who operated a store out of it. The creek divided the town into "Old Town" Sycamore to the north and "New Town" Sycamore to the south. In 1871, the village of Foytown was platted. Six years later, it was absorbed by Sycamore. The combined town of Sycamore was incorporated in 1883.

Marseilles started out as two separate communities about a mile apart. Garrett Fitzgerald of Virginia established Burlington in 1827 while James Robinson of Virginia established Marseilles in 1828. Local businessman Charles Merriman owned the strip of land between the two villages. He sold it to Robinson in 1845. Burlington was soon absorbed, and the combined town became known as Marseilles.

Fowler City was established in 1875 by David Harpster and John Wood and platted two years later. Located along the Columbus & Toledo Railroad, it was named for C.R. Fowler, who owned the land. David Harpster, one of the town's most prosperous residents, was a successful farmer, stock raiser and speculator. Known as the "Wool King," Harpster helped write much of the wool legislation in the nation. The city was renamed Harpster in his honor in June 1890. Colonel Cyrus Sears operated a hotel and post office in the small village.

Nevada, named for the Nevada Territory, was established in 1852 by Jonathan Ayres and Joel Garret, who laid it out along the Pittsburg, Fort Wayne & Chicago Railroad right of way. It was incorporated in 1866. The first person to settle in the limits of present-day Nevada was James McLaughlin, who erected a home in 1849.

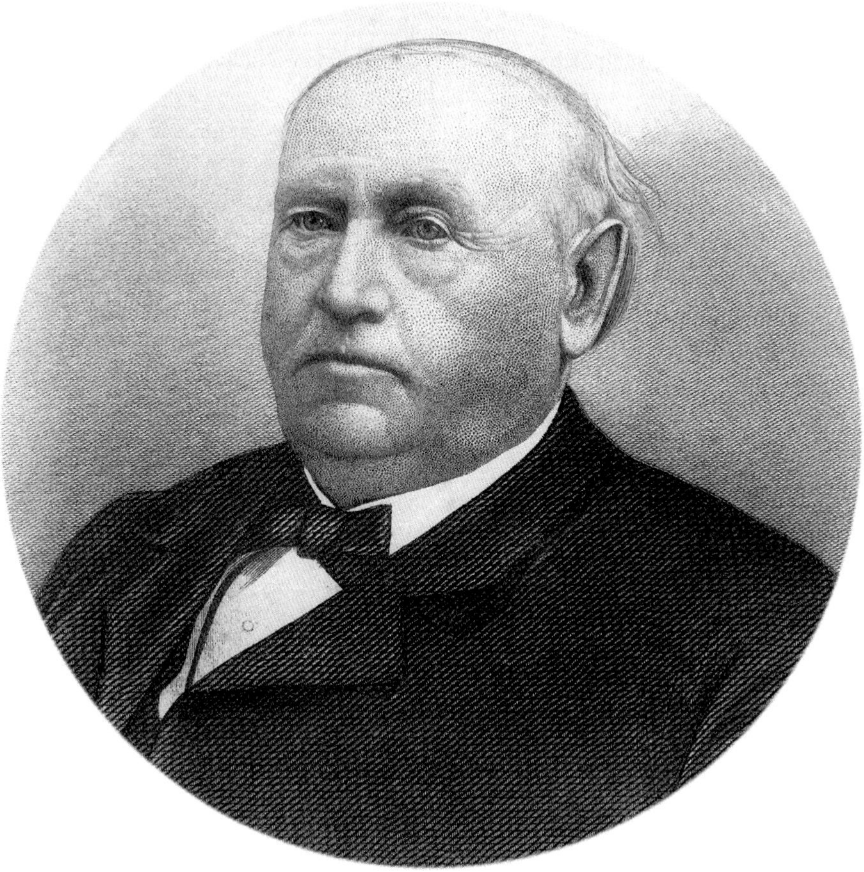

An engraving of David Harpster (1816–1898), who was known as the "Wool King." The town of Fowler City was renamed Harpster in his honor. *Wyandot County Historical Society.*

Numerous smaller communities can be found throughout the county. McCutchenville was platted in June 1829 by Dr. George Sampson on lands owned by Joseph McCutchen, for whom the town was named. The Pervain House was erected by McCutchen in 1829 along the Plank Road to offer weary travelers a place to stop.

Wharton was originally platted as Whartonsburg by Samuel Rathbon in 1848 and named for a local resident. Mexico was platted in 1832 by Thomas Leeper and Hugh Welch. Little Sandusky began life as an Indian trading post and was laid out in 1830 by John Wilson and Dr. Stephen Fowler. The town of Kirby was surveyed by J.H. Williams for Moses H. Kirby in 1854 and laid out along the Pittsburg, Fort Wayne & Chicago Railroad.

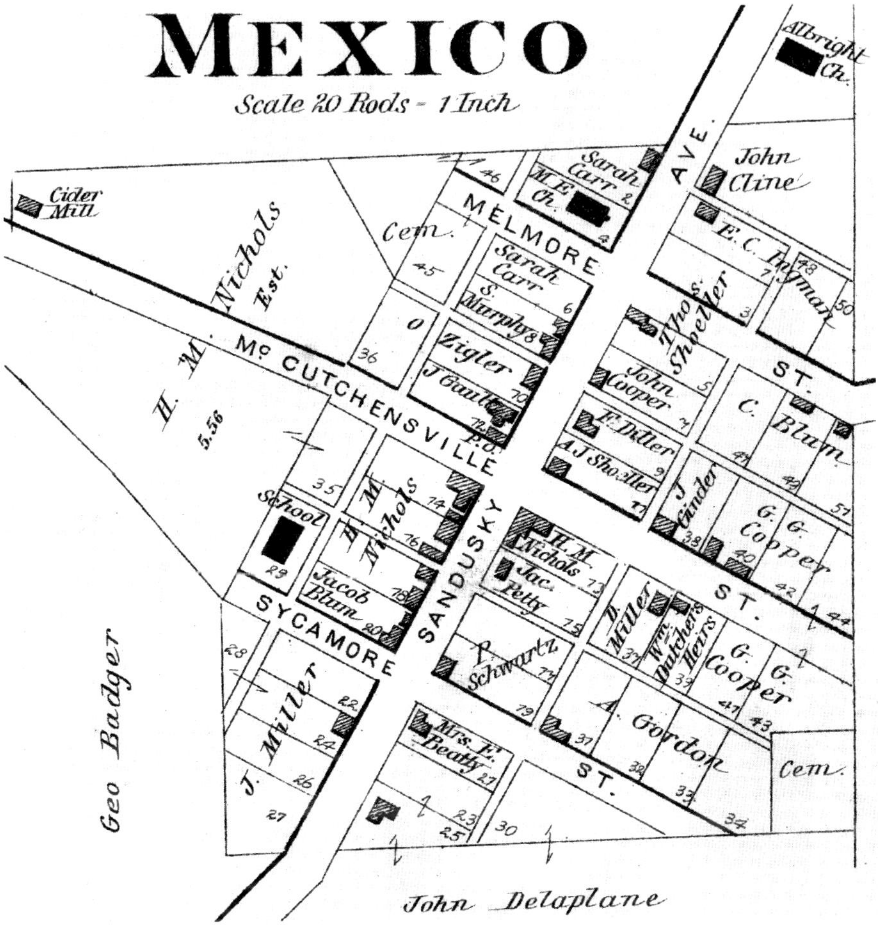

An early plat map for the small community of Mexico located in northeast Tymochtee Township along current County Highway 37. *From* Wyandot County Atlas, *1879.*

Some of the county towns that have shrunk and nearly disappeared from the map are Wyandot, Belle Vernon, Brownstown, Seal, Dunquat, Edenville, Petersburg, Crawfordsville, Lovell, Smithville, Tymochtee, Warpole and Bowsherville. According to the Center for Ghost Town Research in Ohio there are eighty-four ghost towns and semi–ghost towns located within Wyandot County. The group listed three former towns or settlements (Mononcue, Fort Ferree and Adison) within the boundaries of Upper Sandusky.

Many of the early trails through the county were simple paths cut by animals as they migrated through the territory. The numerous native peoples improved these game trails as they hunted and tracked the game. When the

European settlers began to arrive, they followed the narrow trails, eventually widening and smoothing them for use by wagons and buggies. Some of these are the Scioto Trail, the Sandusky Trail and the Wapatomica Trail.

The first attempt to establish a true "road" came about during the War of 1812 when General William Henry Harrison established the "Old War Road." His troops cut out a route that ran from Delaware and passed roughly north–south through the central portion of the county, including Upper Sandusky and the area that would become McCutchenville, extending to Fremont. It was known as the Harrison Trail and follows roughly the same path as present-day U.S. Highway 53.

Shortly after the establishment of Upper Sandusky as the county seat in 1845, plans were begun to create a more permanent road north to Lower Sandusky (Fremont). A plank road running from Columbus to Tiffin was planned in 1848. On March 22, 1849, the Ohio General Assembly passed an act incorporating the Lower Sandusky, Tiffin and Fort Ball Plank Road Company. Wyandot County residents Joseph McCutchen, Robert McKelley and Andrew McElvain were initial subscribers. One year later, on March 23, the Tiffin and Osceola Plank Road Company was incorporated by the state. This action extended the route through Wyandot County to Bucyrus.

The acts provided that the roadbed should be constructed of wood planks at least three inches thick and that the roadway should be at least eight feet

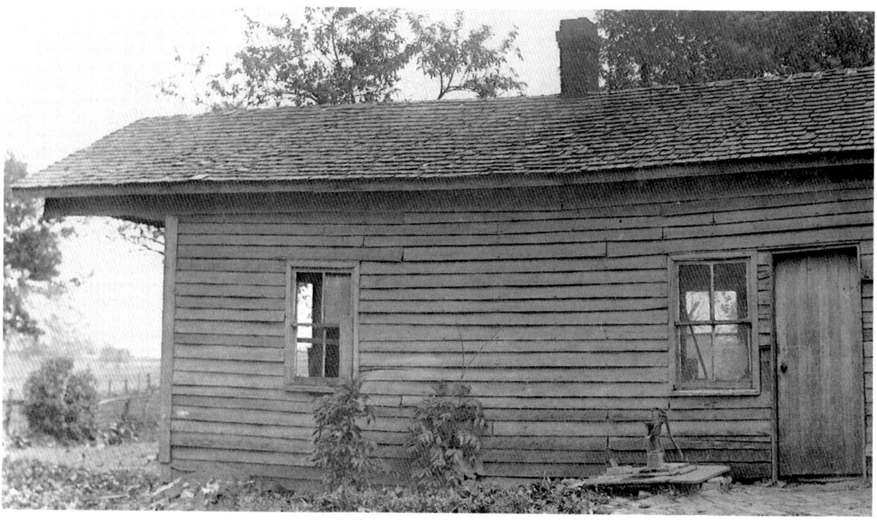

The Lower Sandusky, Tiffin and Fort Ball Plank Road Company's tollhouse stood at the northern edge of Upper Sandusky near the present fairgrounds. *Wyandot County Historical Society.*

wide if single tracked and sixteen feet wide if double tracked. They further decreed that a properly maintained and drained earthen wagon track should be placed alongside the plank road for use by "animals, teams, and travelers of every description." The road appeared like a giant wooden sidewalk extending to the horizon.

The acts also allowed the owners to erect gates and tollhouses after every five miles of plank road was completed. Everyone who used the road or path was required to pay a toll. Upper Sandusky's tollhouse stood near the location of the present fairgrounds. The toll was twelve and a half cents to run a team of horses from Upper Sandusky to Tiffin. After about five years, the roads became too difficult to maintain due to the constantly warping planks. Eventually, the roads were abandoned, planks burned and tollhouses torn down. None of the investors in the plank roads ever made a profit. It would be many more years until gravel pikes would appear in the county.

5

Progress and Development

During the late nineteenth century, the need arose for updated public buildings and utilities. In 1894, a waterworks system, paid for through public bonds, was installed in Carey. The power house and standpipe were located almost a mile from downtown on a site sixty feet higher than the city. Due to gravity and the high water pressure, it afforded sufficient fire protection for Carey. Three years later, the city installed electric lights and combined the electrical plant with the waterworks.

The Upper Sandusky Waterworks Company, operating under a twenty-year franchise granted on April 23, 1889, constructed the waterworks plant alongside the Sandusky River. The original complex included a large brick building housing pumps and machinery, a standpipe and a distributing system tied into pipes subsequently laid through the town. Water was supplied by nearby wells sunk in the gravel banks along the river. Initially, the water was purified through the use of "settling pools," but in 1905, a purification plant was constructed. The plant used two 1.5-million-gallon pumps to send the water through the city water lines and into a 95,000-gallon holding tank. Substantial changes to protect the water supply were required by the state following the Great Flood of 1913, which covered the building up to the roofline. The plant was finally replaced in the 2010s.

As the small villages in the county expanded, they began to experience that most dreaded of maladies for wood frame structures: the fire bug. Small fires in homes or businesses could spread to surrounding structures and create widespread loss. One such fire nearly destroyed the town of

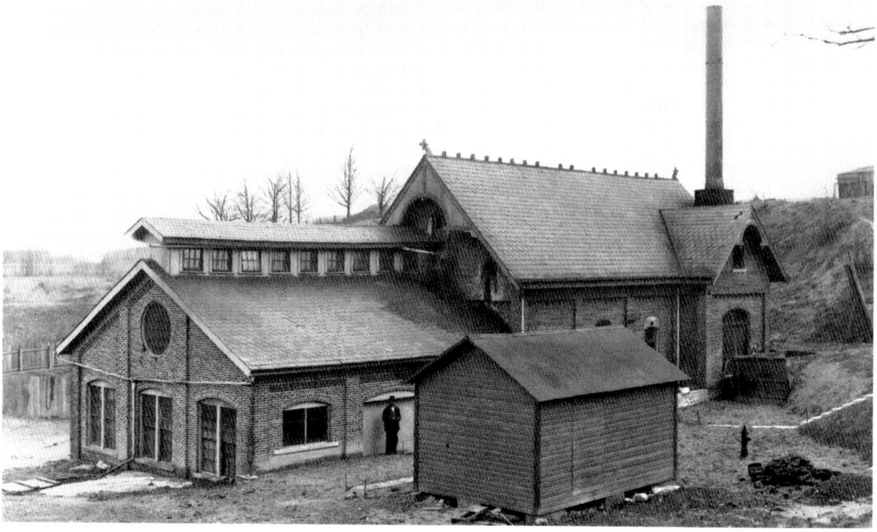

The Upper Sandusky Waterworks was constructed in 1889 along the Sandusky River. The Great Flood of 1913 reached the base of the roofline. *Wyandot County Historical Society*.

Sycamore in June 1877. Local residents began to clamor for the creation of fire brigades.

The first recorded fire company in the county was the Upper Sandusky Fire Department, organized on May 15, 1867, at Allen Kelly's Hall. Sixty men signed up that day. In 1877, the Upper Sandusky citizens purchased the "Wyandot Chief," a steam pumper. By 1884, the department equipment included a hook-and-ladder wagon, two hose carts, 1,500 feet of hose, four ladders and a Babcock chemical engine. Similar volunteer organizations were established in other communities throughout the county in the late 1800s and continue to protect the county residents.

Nevada organized its first fire department on April 8, 1872, with twenty-eight volunteers. Its equipment included a chemical engine, purchased by the town on March 6, 1871, and a Price & Harter hook-and-ladder truck, purchased on January 12, 1872. The town increased its firefighting ability with the purchases of a hand engine named "Water Cloud" and a hose cart from Bucyrus on June 5, 1885.

About 1895, the second courthouse suffered a small fire that destroyed some early records and caused damage to the building. Minor changes were made to stabilize the building, but it was decided to erect a larger "fire-safe" courthouse. At the spring election in 1897, a bond issue to request funds in the amount of $125,000 to construct a new courthouse was placed

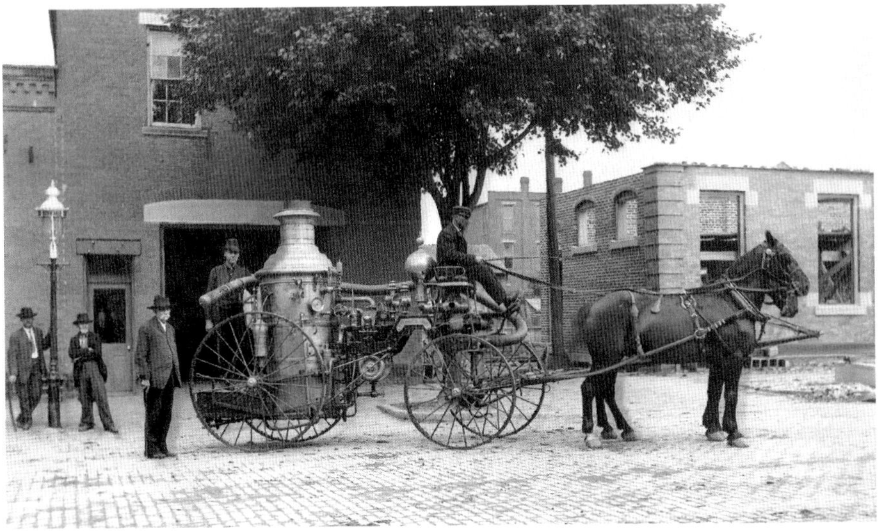

The Wyandot Chief, a horse-drawn steam pump engine, was purchased by the Upper Sandusky Fire Department in 1877. *Wyandot County Historical Society.*

before the public. It was overwhelmingly approved, so the commissioners began the process of replacing the structure. The old building was sold for $10 at public auction on April 24, 1897, to John Laverly, who completely removed it within a month. A small receptacle was found in the cornerstone during demolition. When it was opened, it revealed a deck of cards, an 1847 newspaper and two coins.

The current Wyandot County Courthouse was designed by architects Joseph W. Yost and Frank L. Packard of Columbus. The building was erected between 1897 and 1900 at a cost of $199,740.30. The contract was awarded on July 19, 1897, to C. Boseker & Son of Fort Wayne, Indiana, for the sum of $124,634.97. Two days later, C.E. Richards began construction on the building. The cornerstone was laid by members of Upper Sandusky's Warpole Lodge No. 176, Free & Accepted Masons, on October 18, 1897. The dedication address was given by Judge Allen Smalley of Toledo in front of the nearly ten thousand spectators who attended the ceremony.

The exterior stone used to build the courthouse was quarried from the North Amherst Quarries by the Cleveland Stone Company. It was cut at a depth of one hundred feet below the surface, shipped in large blocks and then dressed and fitted on the construction site. All of the interior marble work was finished and installed by the Evans Marble Company of Baltimore and Chicago. The marble flooring throughout the courthouse came from a quarry in Rutland, Vermont. The tile floor, wainscoting, base work, three-story central stairwell and columns were constructed of East Tennessee marble.

All of the woodwork was quarter-sawn oak made by George R. Butler and Company of Sandusky, Ohio. The fresco work and stained-glass windows were produced by William G. Andrews of Clinton, Iowa. The frescoing cost $7,075 and the stained glass, $1,050. The courthouse's clock tower features four clock faces with announcing bells made by the world-famous Seth Thomas Clock Company at a cost of $2,550.

The courthouse was completed and ready for occupancy on June 23, 1900, and dedicated with much fanfare on August 24. Governor George K. Nash presented the dedication address in front of several thousand attendees. Among the ceremonies was the presentation of the Civil War cannons by General Isaac M. Kirby and the Honorable E.T. Dunn. Because of its historical significance, the Wyandot County Courthouse was listed on the National Register of Historic Places on July 2, 1973.

By the 1880s, the small jail constructed in 1849 had begun to outgrow

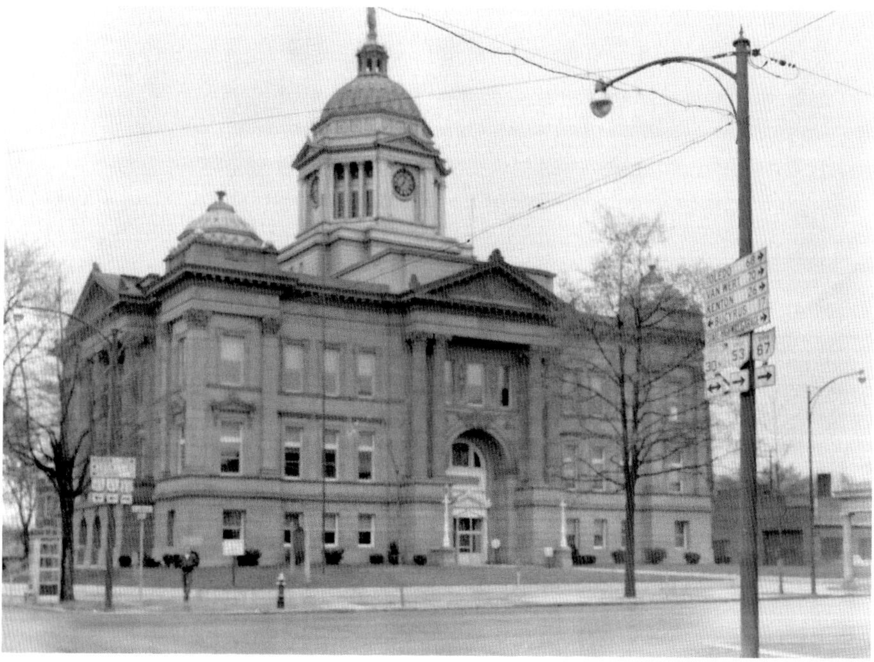

A photograph of the current Wyandot County Courthouse, which was constructed between 1897 and 1900. The roof and domes are currently undergoing restoration. *Wyandot County Historical Society.*

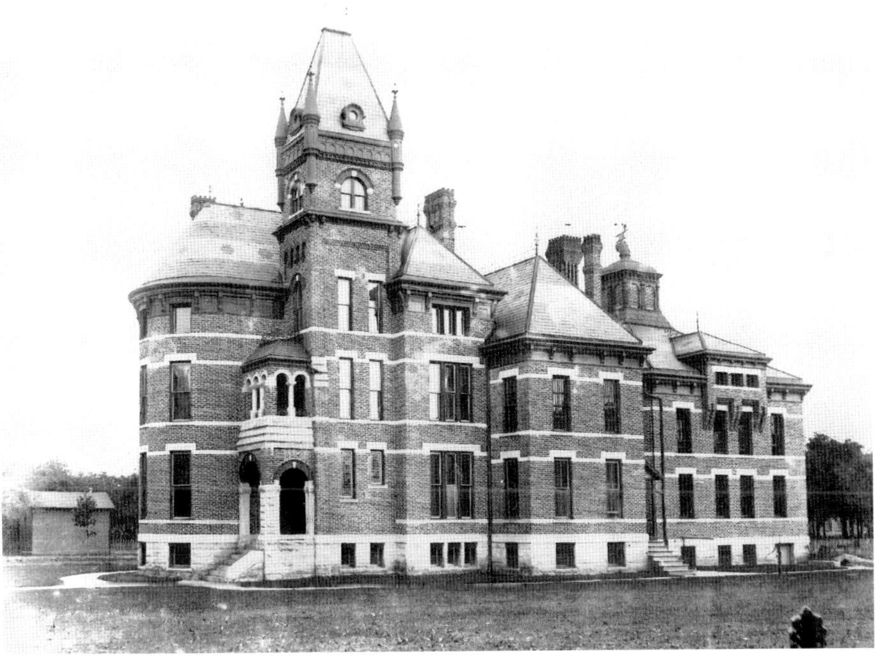

The present Wyandot County Jail was erected in 1888 at a cost of $40,000. It was the third jail to serve the county's residents. *Wyandot County Historical Society.*

its usefulness, so the county decided to commission a new Wyandot County Jail. The commissioners purchased land at the intersection of Fifth Street and Wyandot Avenue, which had previously been the site of the Grundtisch Brothers Carriage Factory, in February 1886. The Queen Anne–style building situated beside the Wyandot County Courthouse was completed in 1888 at a cost of $40,000. The earlier jail was sold at auction in May 1889. The current building was also placed on the National Register of Historic Places on July 2, 1973.

A meeting was held in the Wyandot County Courthouse on December 30, 1848, to secure a railroad through the county. Through an election, $50,000 was raised for the railway, but construction was stopped by a court injunction. Following that order, $15,000 was raised around 1852 to extend the Ohio & Pennsylvania Railroad to Upper Sandusky. The funds paid for tracks, railroad buildings at Upper Sandusky and a bridge over the Sandusky River, built during the summer of 1853. On November 11, 1853, the railroad was completed through Wyandot County into Indiana, forming the new Ohio & Indiana Railroad. The event was celebrated with speeches, patriotic music, the firing of cannons and a formal dinner at the Exchange Hotel. By 1866, this line had been reorganized as the Pittsburg, Fort Wayne & Chicago Railroad Company.

The first train to roll through the county entered Upper Sandusky on November 22, 1853. The occasion was cause for much excitement. Residents reportedly rushed toward the tracks to view the first appearance of the "iron horse." The first passenger train from Pittsburgh arrived on January 20, 1854. It made connections with the Mad River & Lake Erie Railroad heading north to Sandusky City and south to Cincinnati.

The Chesapeake & Ohio Railroad planned tracks through Upper Sandusky to Toledo in 1873 and had completed construction by 1876. The first train to travel over the tracks came through Wyandot County in January 1877. Four years later, the railroad changed its name to the Columbus, Hocking Valley & Toledo Railroad. By the early 1900s, it was simply known as the Hocking Valley Railroad. In 1925, the railway was double-tracked through the county.

Other early railroads to travel through the county were the Cleveland, Cincinnati, Chicago & St. Louis Railroad, known as the "Big Four"; the Toledo & Ohio Central Railroad; and the Northern Ohio Railway, operated by the New York Central Railroad.

Over the years, there have been several train wrecks that caused numerous deaths, injuries and damage to equipment. Some of the early ones were near the towns of Carey (1900 and 1912), Sycamore (1908), Harpster (1910), Nevada (1910) and Upper Sandusky (1932 and 1935). Later wrecks included ones near Nevada (1955), Tymochtee (1966), Carey (1969) and Upper Sandusky (1989).

For several years following the establishment of Wyandot County, the only places to inter bodies were small private family plots or the burial grounds surrounding small churches, such as the Mission Church. This changed in 1866 with the formation of the Nevada Cemetery Association. The original cemetery covered only three acres, but it has been expanded multiple times. The first interment was Elizabeth Andreus Balliet, wife of David Balliet, in September 1866.

In 1874, the citizens of Upper Sandusky began discussing the need for a formal burial ground outside the city. On February 26, 1876, a group of local residents formed the Oak Hill Cemetery Association. They purchased a thirty-acre plot of land overlooking the Sandusky Valley about a mile and a half south of Upper Sandusky. The new cemetery was surveyed, platted and formally dedicated on October 4, 1876. Shortly after this, several of the county towns purchased land

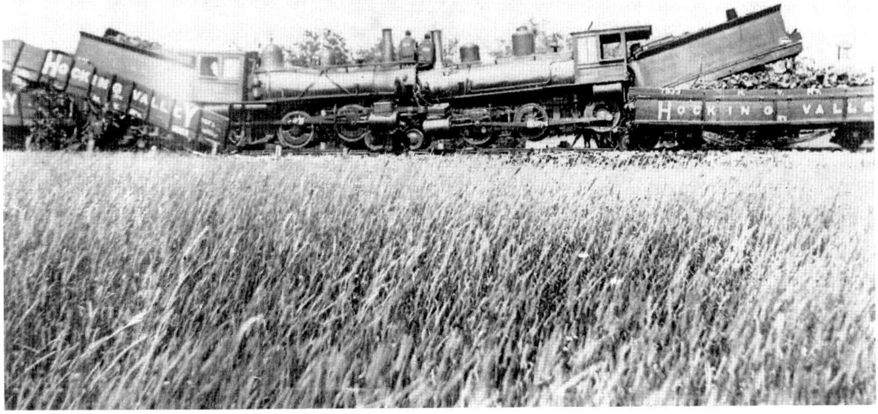

Two trains from the Hocking Valley Railroad crashed head-on in western Wyandot County after one failed to observe a stop signal. *Wyandot County Historical Society.*

for new cemeteries. These include Sycamore Cemetery, Chandler Cemetery near Marseilles and Spring Grove Cemetery near Carey.

Education in the area of Wyandot County began with the Wyandot Mission School in 1821. Many townships erected small log structures in the late 1840s to early 1850s. These were replaced by one-room wood or brick structures in the 1860s and 1870s. The State of Ohio changed the enrollment mandates for local districts about 1910. The ensuing consolidation resulted in ten school districts (Carey, Harpster, Kirby, Marseilles, McCutchenville, Nevada, Salem, Sycamore, Upper Sandusky and Wharton). Consolidation in the 1960s resulted in only three high schools in the county.

The first school in Kirby was erected in 1871. By 1924, there were only six students enrolled, so they were transferred to Wharton High School while Kirby closed. Wharton had several early schools erected in 1870, 1903 and 1922. The last structured burned in 1928, but it was rebuilt and used until 1962, when the school consolidated into the Riverdale School District.

The Nevada Consolidated District was erected in 1917 and constructed a new schoolhouse at the time. This building was expanded in 1934 and 1952 and used until 1961, when Nevada was consolidated into the Wynford School District. The first brick schoolhouse was erected in Harpster about 1875. A second building was built in 1917 and used until consolidating in the Upper Sandusky School District.

In 1915, the McCutchenville Rural School District was established. It consisted of five buildings until 1923, when a brick structure was erected for the high school. This was used until the school consolidated into the Sycamore Mohawk School District. The Sycamore Special School District was formed in 1885 following the erection of a new brick schoolhouse, which was replaced in 1911 and used until a fire consumed the building in 1940. Two years later, the school was rebuilt and used until the creation of the Sycamore Mohawk School District in 1957.

The first schoolhouse erected in Marseilles was in 1823, followed by a frame structure in 1837 and a brick building in 1847. The Marseilles School District was formed in 1875, and a brick school was constructed two years later. This building was used until consolidation with Upper Sandusky in 1962.

The longest-operating school district in the county is the Upper Sandusky School District, which traces its history to 1854 when it erected the brick Union School. A series of schoolhouses were erected, culminating with the Upper Sandusky High School in 1962. The Carey School District began roughly with the erection of two small log schoolhouses in 1843. Later buildings were erected in 1855, 1868, 1887, 1904 and 1929. The main portion of the current high school was erected in 1921 and added to several times. The school district is in the process of constructing a new high school slated to open by 2016.

Religion has been a large part of Wyandot County's history beginning with John Stewart's missionary work and continuing with the construction of numerous churches throughout the county. The only one of these new churches that has acquired world renown is Carey's National Shrine to Our Lady of Consolation—or St. Mary's Shrine, as it is sometimes called.

Father Edward Vatmann of Findlay supervised the construction of the first church in Carey in 1868. Once the building was completed enough for use, it was dedicated and named St. Edward Church with Father Joseph Peter Gloden in charge. He encouraged the congregation to raise funds to complete the building with prayers given to Mary under the title of Our Lady of Consolation. Father Joseph promised to rename the church in honor of Our Lady of Consolation upon its completion. It soon became known as the National Shrine of Our Lady of Consolation, or St. Mary's Shrine.

A replica of the statue of Our Lady of Consolation revered in the Cathedral of Luxembourg was procured from Luxembourg for the new church. On May 24, 1875, the statue was carried in a formal procession from the Church of St. Nicholas in Frenchtown to the church in Carey. According to oral tradition, there was a terrible storm the day of the procession, but not a

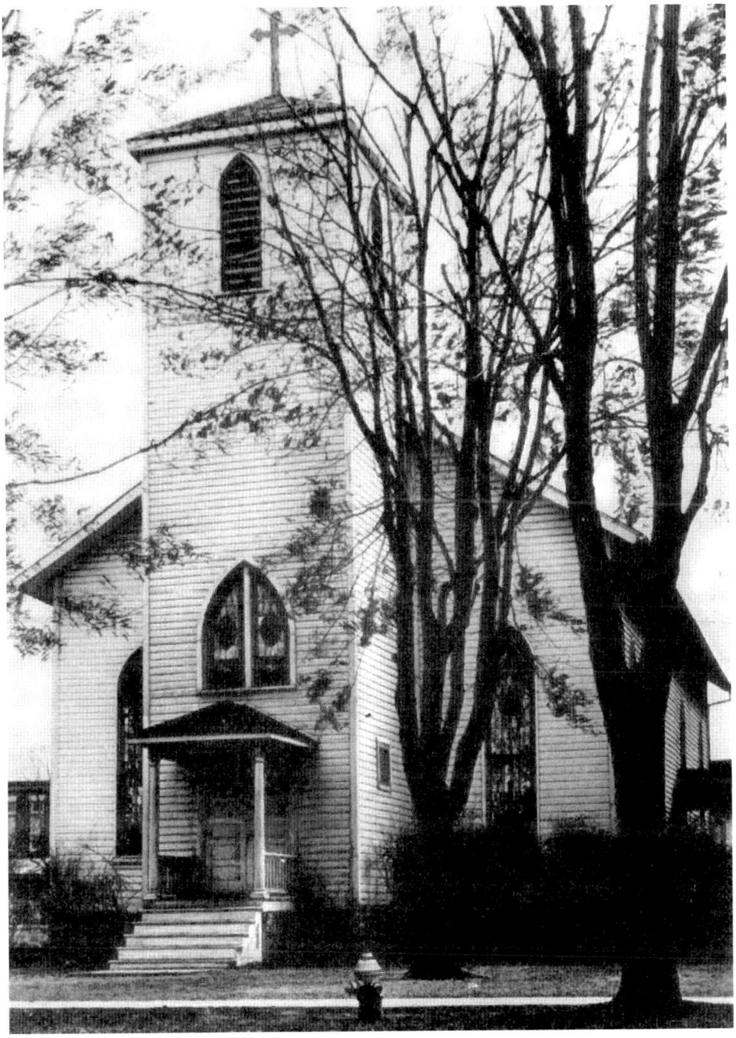

The original building of the National Shrine of Our Lady of Consolation in Carey was begun in 1866 by Father Edward Vatmann. *Wyandot County Historical Society.*

drop of rain fell on the statue. Franciscan friars arrived in Carey during 1912 to care for the countless pilgrims who visited the shrine. Three blocks from the shrine is a park containing a memorial altar that was dedicated in 1957 and the twenty-three Stations of the Cross.

The Wyandottes were relocated to Kansas in 1843, and the Indian Mill saw sparing use by local millers, such as Michael Ruch and Josiah Lowry,

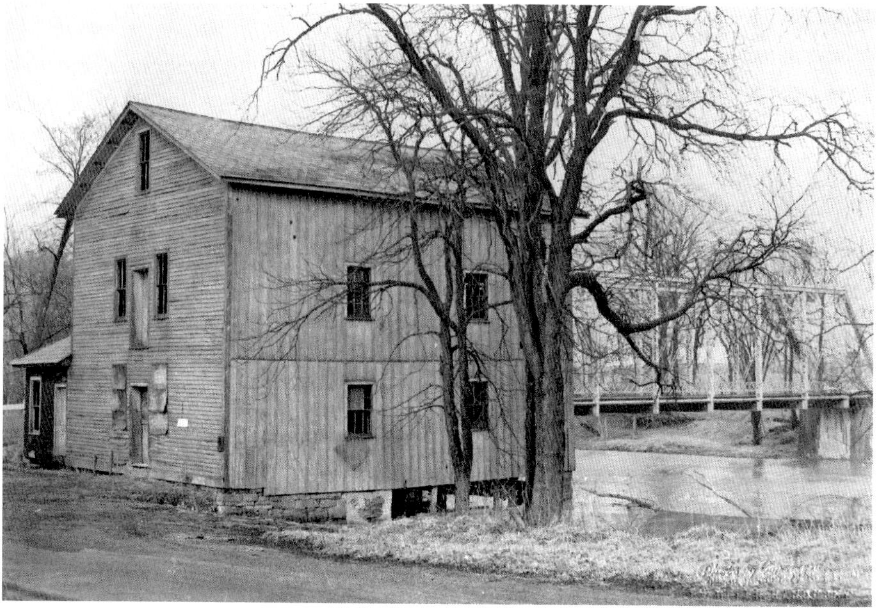

The somewhat dilapidated Indian Mill as it appeared in the late 1910s. The Finkle family operated the mill from 1885 until 1943. *Wyandot County Historical Society.*

until George Myers took over operations in 1848. In 1861, Meyers had former government miller Louis Rummel build a new mill using lumber salvaged from the former grist- and sawmills. It was built in a fairly unique Howe truss style, normally only seen in covered bridges, making it strong enough to withstand the constant shaking associated with the grinding. Eric Sloan, the famous woodworking tool expert and author, once wrote to a previous curator that he had seen the way the main beams were pinned together used only in railroad trestle construction, thereby adding another layer of strength to the building.

By 1865, David Maxwell was operating the mill, and in 1872, he sold it to Isaac Mann, who operated it as a flour mill. About the time John Finkle acquired the mill in 1885 for $2,000, the water level in the Sandusky River had significantly lowered so that he could grind only cornmeal efficiently. It stayed in the Finkle family until 1943, when Foster Finkle ceased operations at the mill and sold the building to Ward Walton. Eventually, it would be transformed into a milling museum.

The Wyandot County Agriculture Society was organized on January 3, 1852, at the Wyandot County Courthouse. There were 129 members present at this first meeting, and that number has increased to over 800 members today. The first Wyandot County Fair was actually held the previous year (1851) on the Thompson Farm, currently the site of the Fairhaven Community on Marseilles Avenue in Upper Sandusky. The fair was held at the farm site until 1856, when the current fairgrounds were purchased. This site, north of town, was originally eighteen acres. Between 1861 and 1920, an additional thirty-nine acres were purchased by the Agriculture Society to expand the grounds.

The first racetrack was built at the fairgrounds in 1859. It was expanded from a one-third-mile to a half-mile track in 1873 and replaced by the current racetrack in 1921. The first grandstands were erected in 1906, rebuilt in 1921 and raised in 1988. The present one was erected the next year. In 1921, all fair buildings were moved to the east side of the grounds. A caretaker's house was erected in 1952. The Secretary's Office, formerly the Steck Grocery and Henry Miller Restaurant, was moved to the fairgrounds in 1967. In 2014, the Wyandot County Agricultural Society held its 163rd consecutive fair.

The original Pioneer Log Cabin was located on the fairgrounds. Built by local residents, it was completed on June 11, 1888. It was constructed of logs donated from every township in the county. The cabin originally faced northwest with the fireplace on the southwest end. The building contained two small rooms with an open foyer between them. It was filled with pioneer relics, many of which were later placed in the new Wyandot County Museum at the courthouse. The building was moved twice and the fireplace removed completely after the final move. The building served its purpose until falling into disrepair in the 1990s. Considered unsafe, funds were raised to erect a new structure. The current Pioneer Log Cabin was dedicated on June 11, 2000.

During the 1800s, horse-drawn vehicles were used for nearly every transportation need. Whether it was hauling stone and wood for bridge construction, riding into and around town or delivering food and groceries, there was a specific type of vehicle constructed. Between about 1850 and 1915, there were well over fifty different buggy, wagon and carriage manufacturers operating in the county. Every town (large and small) and even remote townships had wagon builders or at least a blacksmith or wheelwright who could repair them.

Henry G. Lea established his blacksmith shop in August 1863 along Nevada's Morrison (Main) Street, just south of the railroad. Four years later, he added carriage and wagon manufacturing, naming it the H.G. Lea Carriage Shop. His sons, William and Frank, joined the business in May 1888, leading

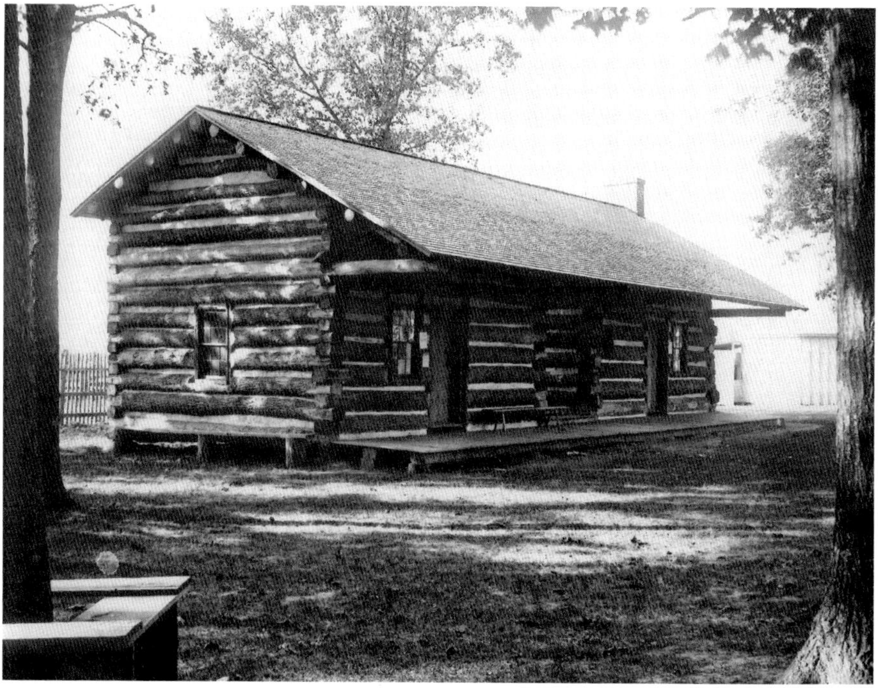

The two-room Pioneer Log Cabin was constructed using local logs on the county fairgrounds in June 1888 by volunteers. *Wyandot County Historical Society.*

to the obvious name H.G. Lea and Sons. The company created and sold the "famous" Lea Road Cart worldwide. By 1895, the shop had ceased operations.

William McClelland worked in his father's blacksmith shop in Patterson, Ohio, before moving to Whartonsburg. He was employed by P.R. Moore for three years before opening his own blacksmith shop along the north side of Sandusky Street. He advertised that he manufactured and repaired all types of farm wagons. In 1882, he partnered with W.K. Voegel, forming the firm of McClelland and Voegel. Near the end of the 1890s, he closed this shop and moved to Marion County.

Henry Huffsey opened his first carriage shop in Seneca County about 1870. He received a patent with William H. Keppler for a horse-drawn vehicle improvement on June 27, 1871. He moved to Sycamore in the mid-1870s, where he set up a carriage shop at the corner of Sycamore and Fifth Streets. The shop manufactured carriages, buggies and spring wagons while repairing all types of horse-drawn vehicles. In 1902, his blacksmith and wagon shop was located at 101 West Fifth Street, where he worked until his death in 1913.

Frank Tripp established his first blacksmith shop in 1845. After serving during the Civil War, he returned to Upper Sandusky and opened another blacksmith shop in 1864. Six years later, he added carriage and wagon making, naming the new business the Frank Tripp Carriage and Wagon Works. His son, Allen, joined the firm during the 1870s. Frank invented and patented "Tripp's Buckeye Wagon Tongue Support" in 1883. The new improvement sold well and was adapted by other buggy makers. The shop closed about 1890, and two years later, the Gordon Casket Company remodeled the old shop buildings for their new use.

Perhaps the best-known and longest-lasting carriage maker in Wyandot County was John J. Seider. He arrived in Upper Sandusky in 1852 and learned the trade under carriage maker William Bearinger for four years. Seider established his own shop in 1856 for $150 and began making small wagons and oxcarts. He formed a partnership with David E. Hale in 1865 under the name of Hale & Seider. During the 1870s, he bought out Hale's interest and partnered with Frank M. Beidler in the firm Seider & Beidler. Following Beidler's retirement in 1880, Peter S. Ludwig joined, creating the new firm of Seider & Ludwig.

John Seider became the sole proprietor in 1884 and established the John Seider Carriage Works, which manufactured nearly all types of horse-drawn vehicles, including buggies, carriages, spring wagons, farm wagons and sleighs. His sons, John J. and Edward F., joined him about 1900, forming the Seider & Sons Carriage and Wagon Shop. As "horseless carriages" began to appear more frequently in the mid-1900s, the enterprising Seider was one of the first local shops to offer paint, trim and repair services for automobiles. Edward became proprietor and general manager upon the death of his father in 1921. He closed the business about two years later.

One of the more interesting individuals to live in Wyandot County during the late 1800s was Alexander W. Brinkerhoff, the celebrated merchant and inventor. He was born on March 4, 1821, in Gettysburg, Pennsylvania, and moved with his family to McCutchenville in May 1834. At the age of twenty, he learned the trades of cabinetmaking and carpentry. He began clerking in a McCutchenville store until attending college. He taught school until opening a dry goods store that operated for seven years in Sycamore with J.B. Wilson. In 1857, he moved to Upper Sandusky, where he began to market and sell his inventions. Alexander partnered with his son, Milford, in 1869 to operate a store selling queensware, organs and sewing machines. He organized the Ohio Fruit Jar Company on March 27, 1876, to sell his "Patent Self-Sealing Fruit Jars."

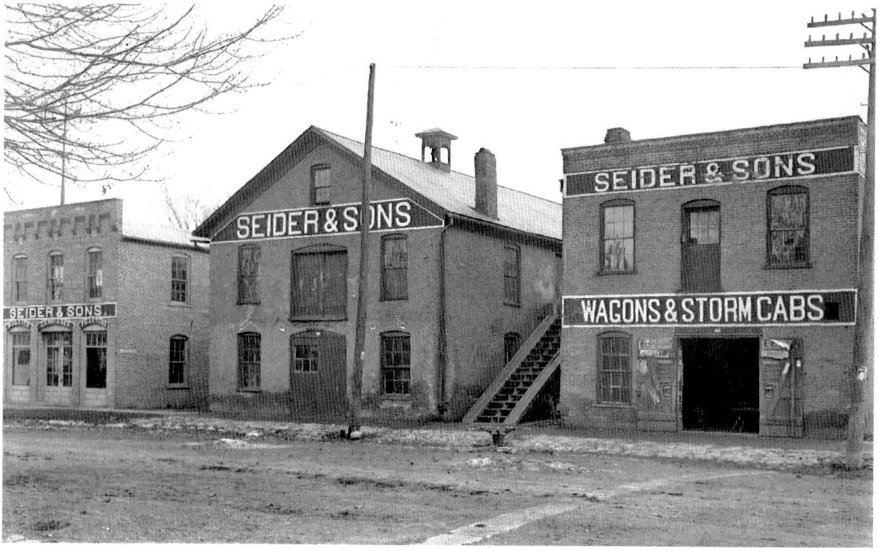

The brick Seider and Sons Carriage and Wagon Shop buildings were erected by John Seider about 1906–07 along East Walker Street. *Wyandot County Historical Society.*

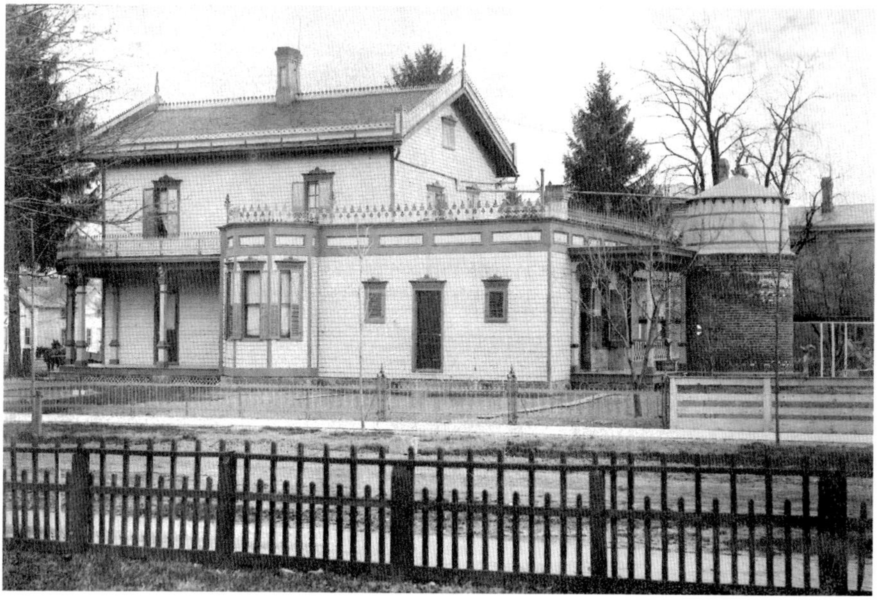

Alexander W. Brinkerhoff's home along East Wyandot Avenue in Upper Sandusky is where he originally envisioned and designed several of his inventions. *Wyandot County Historical Society.*

An inventor, he redesigned many utilitarian items and created several new items. He was not limited to one area, as he tinkered with items from the medical, housewares, business and agricultural fields. Some of the items he invented or upgraded were the Ohio Fruit Jar, the commonsense ink stand, brass cornhuskers, corn planters, the clothespin, syringes, the operating needle, the speculum, the operating table and the tobacco pouch. The first county resident to receive a patent (1856), he continued to introduce new items into the 1880s. Brinkerhoff died in Upper Sandusky on March 13, 1887. He was credited with over thirty inventions and held over two dozen patents during his lifetime.

While researching, it was easy to find fun tidbits of history, and I've included a few from the nineteenth century. President James Monroe, General Duncan McArthur and Ohio governor Thomas Worthington reportedly stayed at the Garrett Tavern. Governor (later President) Rutherford B. Hayes passed through the county in February 1877. Other early presidents to visit the county were the aforementioned William H. Harrison in 1812, Robert Taft in 1912 and Warren Harding, who reportedly met his mistress in a secret location near the Indian Mill.

George Duddleston, a local teamster, used a 715-pound wagon constructed by Frank Tripp to transport 8,215 pounds of stone in one trip from the depot to the Indian Mill Bridge in July 1871. A rat hunt in 1890 exterminated over 21,500 rats in just thirty days. In February 1891, the Standard Oil Company headquarters were briefly located in Lovell. Two baseball teams from Toledo and Columbus dared to play a Sunday baseball game in Upper Sandusky in 1894. Twenty-one persons were arrested and given over ninety-six dollars in fines. Despite all this, the game went off peacefully.

6

A New Century

As the twentieth century dawned, many exciting, progressive changes were soon to come to the United States, and Wyandot County was no exception. From the first cross-country highway to a nearly-forgotten landmark court case to the "War to End All Wars," the county had a hand in it all. Much more occurred during the first half of the 1900s than can possibly be written in these few pages, so the following are highlights of how Wyandot County impacted Ohio and the nation.

One of the first and most important court cases to take place in the newly constructed Wyandot County Courthouse was that of the so-called Findlay Gang, a group of highwaymen and bank robbers, who were charged with the murder of William Johnson. On March 6, 1901, the grand jury indicted five men for first-degree murder (Charles Foster, Willis Miller, Marsh Lindsay, George Ury and Locke Foster), while declining to indict Eugene Hames.

Johnson, known as the "Celery King," operated the Wild Rose Celery Farm north of Carey. It was extremely prosperous due to the fertile, black muck soil in the area. He was rumored to keep large amounts of cash in his home. The Findlay Gang heard these stories, including one that he had recently sold a large crop, and decided to pay Johnson a late-night visit on September 11, 1900. Shortly after the gang's arrival, it was apparent that there was little to no money in the home as the farmer had recently made a deposit. Only a few dollars and a watch were received from Johnson. Frustrated, one of the men shot him in front of his wife and family, who had been tied up.

Five separate trials were held in 1901, in which Johnson's wife, Alma, and the couple's three children testified. To ensure that the other men would receive a fair trial, Judge Boston G. Young issued an order before the first trial restricting the publication of any testimony from the first trial in local newspapers. The Scripps-McRae League (similar to today's Associated Press) sued to get this order overturned. Despite several appeals and other legal attempts, the judge's ruling was eventually upheld by the Supreme Court. This was one of the first rulings like this in the country and paved the way for the gag orders of today.

All five men were subsequently convicted, most sentenced to life in prison, although none served longer than thirteen years. Charles Foster, their reported leader, was the first to be tried and died in jail less than two years after his sentencing. Miller and Lindsay also reportedly died in prison. Based on conflicting stories by witnesses, Guy was approved for a pardon by the State Board of Pardons in 1911. However, Governor Judson Harmon refused to grant his release. It was not until June 1913 that he was pardoned by Governor James M. Cox and released from prison. Locke Foster, the third man to be tried, was also pardoned by Governor Cox in May 1914.

Several sensational court cases took place in Wyandot County during the 1930s, including the murder of Grace Bowers by her husband in 1932 and the killing of R.V. Brown in 1933. Robert Vernon Brown was a traveling showman who specialized in exhibiting Native American artifacts excavated from graves and former village sites. He was born in Belmont County, Ohio, on June 15, 1881. Formerly a marshal in Powhatan Point, Ohio, Brown considered himself an amateur archaeologist and traveled around in an old bus showing off his collections in a touring medicine show and Indian relic exhibition.

It was during one of his many tours of Ohio that he met Eva Timmer. She was a forty-two-year-old, single mother from Ferndale, Michigan, who had previously worked as a lecturer, carnival worker and fortuneteller. They decided to form a partnership with her as the booker and promoter. During a trip through West Virginia and southern Ohio in October 1933, she reportedly killed Brown.

Two different stories arose as to how Brown was murdered. Timmer told Sheriff Harry Weatherholtz that Brown had tried to attack her as they stopped in southern Ohio and that she had killed him in self-defense. She added that she had stuffed Brown's body in the back of the bus and driven around Ohio for several hours before dumping the body near Carey on October 13. The coroner's inquest uncovered that the body

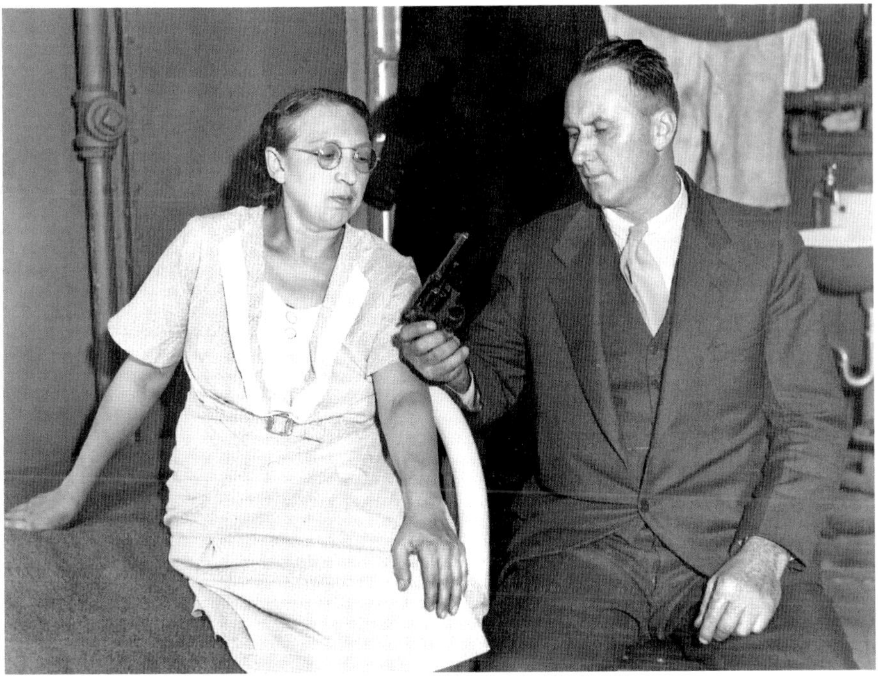

Accused murderess Eva Timmer and Sheriff Harry Weatherholtz examine the revolver she reportedly used to murder Robert V. Brown in 1933. *Wyandot County Historical Society.*

was apparently still warm when discovered, contradicting her story. It was later determined that Brown had been bludgeoned with a flatiron (on display in the Wyandot County Museum) and shot through the head shortly before being discovered. She was found guilty of manslaughter at her trial and sentenced to the Ohio Reformatory for Women. Timmer was later transferred to the Lima State Hospital, from where she escaped on the night of November 21, 1940, never to be seen or heard from again.

In the summer of 1907, the *Cycle and Automobile Trade Journal* announced the debut of a new Model A "gasolene" runabout from the U.S. (United States) Motor Car Company in Upper Sandusky. The steel and hickory wood machine weighed 1,400 pounds and sported a twelve-horsepower motor capable of attaining speeds of up to thirty-five miles an hour. It was available in a dark green finish with soft cushions on the seats. The price was $900, which included a full toolkit, a tire repair kit and a pump. The new vehicle was due to be put in production in 1908 but lasted only one year. Information on the company is scarce, and it is unclear exactly how long the company existed and how many vehicles were actually produced. It

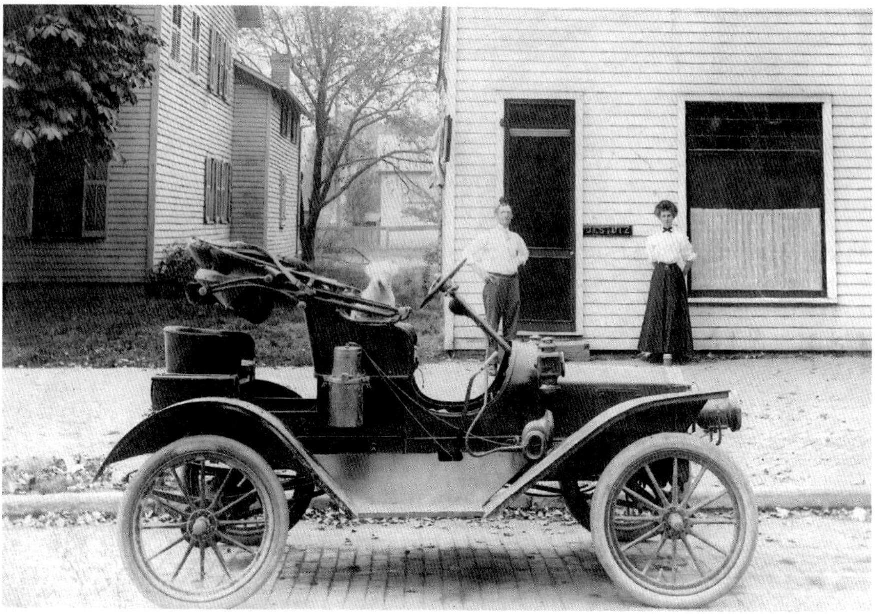

Dr. Otto C. Stutz and his wife, Cora, pose with his car in front of the physician's office. He began his practice in 1885. *Wyandot County Historical Society.*

is thought the factory burned sometime late in 1908 or early 1909, ending production of the only motor vehicle ever known to be manufactured in Wyandot County. During the early 1900s, several prominent residents began driving "horseless carriages" throughout the county.

In September 1912, Carl G. Fisher, president of Prest-O-Lite Company in Indianapolis, Indiana, conceived the idea of constructing a "hard-surfaced, improved highway" from the Atlantic Ocean to the Pacific. He called his idea the "Coast-to-Coast Rock Highway," and it was Fisher's hope that he would find financial support from leaders of the automotive industry to build this first transcontinental automobile route. Later that same year, Henry B. Joy, president of Packard Motor Car Company, would propose to Fisher that this new highway also serve as a memorial to the nation's beloved fallen president, Abraham Lincoln.

As an "appeal to patriots," Joy's idea was well-received, and on July 1, 1913, in Detroit, Michigan, the Lincoln Highway Association was officially organized, with Joy being elected its first president. On October 31, 1913, the Lincoln Highway was officially dedicated. Towns and cities all across America, including Wyandot County, celebrated with torchlight parades, bonfires, speeches, dances, fireworks and cannon fire.

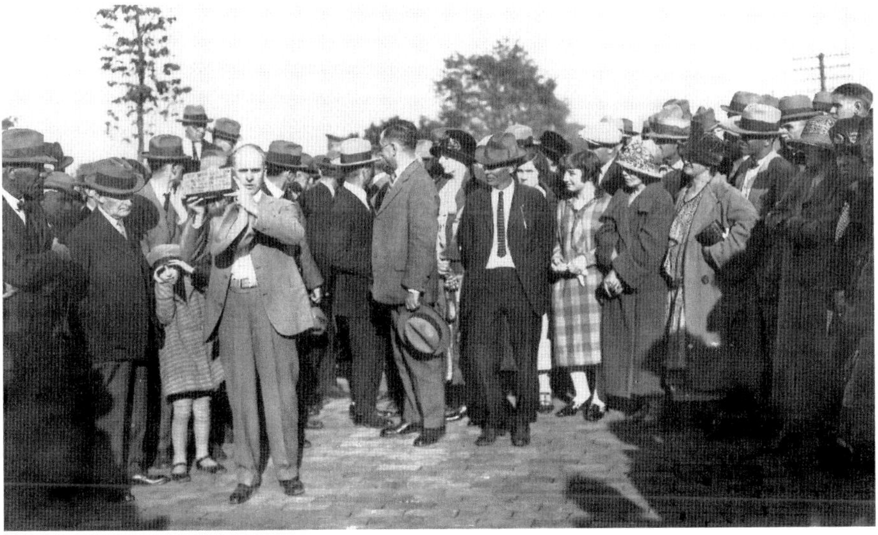

George F. Schlesinger holds the official last brick for the seven-mile Lincoln Highway paving project between Bucyrus and Upper Sandusky in August 1925. *Wyandot County Historical Society.*

The 1913–19 routes entered the county from the east along County Highway 182 toward Nevada and continued into Upper Sandusky. The route west originally "zigzagged" out of town along State Route 53 toward Forest in Hardin County. In June 1919, the Lincoln Highway bypassed Nevada and Upper Sandusky for a much straighter path across the county along County Highway 330 from Oceola toward the western border.

In 1925, the State of Ohio finalized a contract to pave roughly seven miles of the Lincoln Highway with Ohio-made bricks. The route began in Upper Sandusky continuing through the eastern part of Wyandot County to Bucyrus in Crawford County. The last brick was placed by State of Ohio director of highways George F. Schlesinger during dedication ceremonies on August 23, 1925.

Millions of vehicles have traveled across the Lincoln Highway, but perhaps the most interesting one was the Antarctic Snow Cruiser in 1939. The vehicle was designed and built by Dr. Thomas C. Poulter between 1937 and 1939 to aid in Admiral Richard Byrd's exploration of Antarctica and was equipped to carry a Beechcraft D17A Staggerwing aircraft secured on top. It measured around fifty-six feet long by twelve feet wide and sixteen feet high. Surprisingly, it was equipped with ten-foot-high, treadless swamp buggy–style tires to traverse the icy breadth of Antarctica. Following its construction, the cruiser (sans aircraft) was driven along the Lincoln Highway from Chicago to Boston, where it would be loaded for its long voyage to Antarctica.

Shortly before its arrival in Wyandot County, the vehicle ran off the highway near Gomer, causing minor damage. On November 1, 1939, the Antarctic Snow Cruiser made an appearance in downtown Upper Sandusky. Needing hydraulic line repairs, it was delayed here for five hours. Following the arrival of parts from Chicago, Dewey Dillon of Upper Auto Parts was contracted to machine out a fitting necessary to complete the repairs. During this delay, local schools and businesses were closed to allow everyone the chance to view this extremely large machine, resulting in a large crowd that gathered in front of the Lutheran church on West Wyandot Avenue. Following repairs, it continued its journey, finally arriving in Boston on November 12. Last seen in 1958, it is unknown whether the Cruiser is simply buried under ice and snow or sitting on the bottom of the Southern Ocean following the break-up of the Ross Ice Shelf.

Throughout the years, there have been numerous floods reported along the Sandusky River and its tributaries. The most disastrous flood to ever occur in Wyandot County was the Great Flood of 1913. Following heavy rains between March 23 and 27, the Sandusky River rose as much as forty-five feet above the normal water level. Upper Sandusky recorded a little over ten inches of rain that week with three and a half inches recorded on the twenty-fifth. Rivers throughout the county rose out of their banks, covering the land, making it appear that the Great Swamp was reclaiming its territory.

Luckily, compared with other counties in the state, Wyandot suffered relatively little damage and no loss of life. Several small bridges were damaged or washed downstream, the most notable being the old covered bridge erected in 1861 beside the Indian Mill. The Pennsylvania Railroad through the county suffered loss of track due to the water's washing away the banks that supported the rails.

Evidence of the waters was everywhere. Farmers' fields, as well as streets in Carey, were under several feet of water. The Indian Mill had as much as ten feet of water in the building, and Harrison Smith Park was inundated by about thirty feet of water, nearly reaching the bottom of the railroad trestle along the south side. The biggest impact to the residents of Upper Sandusky was the flooding of the waterworks, which was situated alongside the river. The retention ponds were submerged by water contaminated with debris and raw sewage from towns along the river and its tributaries. The pumps were out for two weeks, and when they were able to restart them,

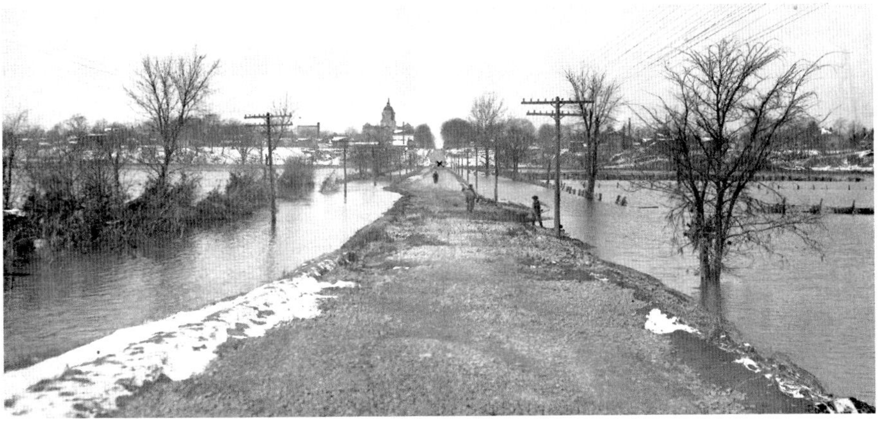

Looking west up Kirby Hill following the Great Flood of 1913. Six months later, the dirt-covered Wyandot Avenue became part of the Lincoln Highway. *Wyandot County Historical Society.*

the city declared a "boil water" alert for another eleven days. Eventually, the waters receded, but this event was memorialized as one of the greatest natural disasters to strike the county.

One of the greatest symbols of America, the Liberty Bell, has appeared in Wyandot County twice during its cross-country tours. In 1893, the Liberty Bell traveled from Philadelphia across the Pennsylvania Railroad to Chicago for the World's Columbian Exposition. It passed through the towns of Upper Sandusky, Nevada and Kirby without much fanfare or recognition on April 28, 1893. The second time it came through the county was in 1915, when it traveled from Philadelphia to San Francisco to be exhibited at the Panama-Pacific International Exposition.

The 1915 trip was the last cross-country tour for the famous bell following several earlier tours to regional expositions and world fairs. Over 500,000 schoolchildren in California signed a petition requesting that the Liberty Bell visit the West Coast. To protect the fragile bell, a special seven-car train was created to support and transport it during its long journey. The "Liberty Bell Special," with forty escorts and armed guards, traveled primarily along the route of the Pennsylvania Railroad.

It departed Philadelphia on July 5, 1915, with the first major stop scheduled at Mansfield, Ohio, at 7:25 a.m. on July 6. It was due to arrive in Upper Sandusky at 8:50 a.m.; however, it arrived about fifteen minutes late due to the large demand of viewers seeking a glimpse of the bell along the route. During its stop here, Frank B. Stockley of the Common Council of Philadelphia gave an address about the bell to the children in attendance.

According to the July 6, 1915 issue of the *Wyandot Union-Republican* (Upper Sandusky) nearly five thousand persons turned out to see the Liberty Bell in Upper Sandusky. Only one person, Virginia Smith, the young daughter of Mr. and Mrs. Philip Smith, was permitted to touch the Liberty Bell during its visit in Wyandot County. The bell also passed through Nevada, Kirby and Forest, although it is not known to have stopped in any other town.

The next extended stop was scheduled for Lima after it traveled through and briefly stopped (usually for about five minutes) at small towns along the route. Other northwestern Ohio towns along the railroad where the train officially stopped were Crestline, Bucyrus, Upper Sandusky, Dunkirk, Ada and Van Wert. The train briefly stopped in Dunkirk so Ohio governor Frank Willis could hop on board and triumphantly accompany the bell into his hometown of Ada. After traveling through thirty states, the Liberty Bell returned to Philadelphia on November 25, 1915, and has resided in the city ever since.

The Dorcas Carey Public Library traces its history back to the Woman's Christian Temperance Union in the late 1800s. The ladies amassed a small collection of books, which were given to the Carey High School Literary Club. The addition of numerous volumes by W.T. Dickerson led to the creation of the Dickerson Public Library, which was supported financially by the local board of education for a few years. A tax levy provided funds for the library and generated interest in a public library separate from the high school.

Andrew Carnegie announced plans in 1904 to set aside a portion of his wealth to support the creation of public libraries across the nation. Shortly after, Mayor Greely Chambers arranged for Carey to receive funding from the philanthropist in the amount of $8,000. Edwin Brown contributed another $5,000 toward the library. This included the amount needed to purchase the building lot, which was at one time the location of the Samuel Lytle Blacksmith and Wagon Shop. The new building was completed in 1906 with the dedication taking place at Snyder's Opera House on October 19. It was named the Dorcas Carey Public Library in honor of the wife of Judge John Carey, founder of Carey.

The library was not remodeled until 1967. Then, in 1976, $6,000 was donated toward the construction of an addition to the original building. A tax levy the next year provided additional funds to begin the construction, which was completed in October 1979. Arthur Stoll bequeathed $50,000 in 1985 to the Dorcas Carey Public Library to add a second floor to the 1979 addition. The new level was completed in 1987 and marked the last

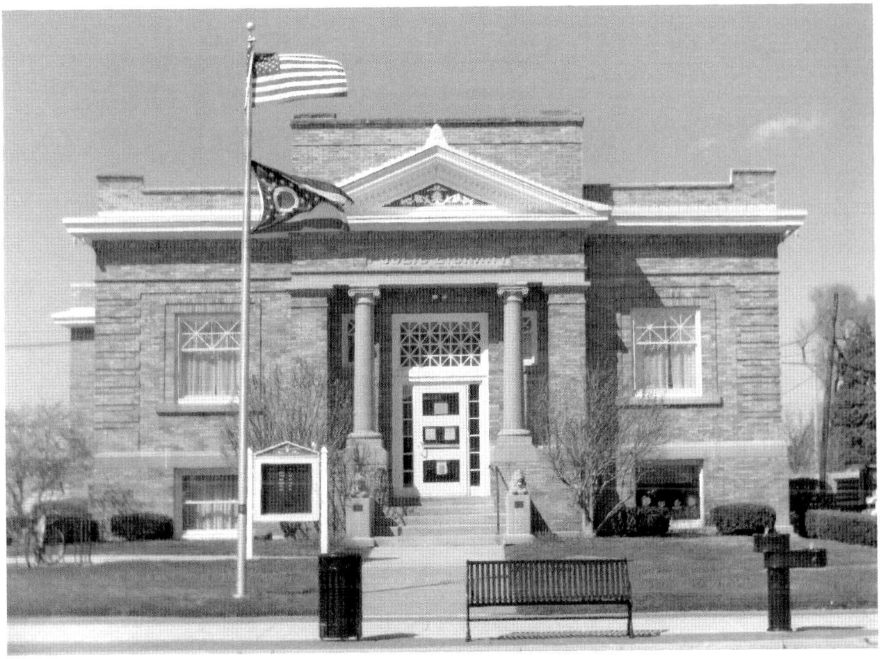

The original Dorcas Carey Library was completed in 1906, primarily with funds from philanthropist Andrew Carnegie, and has been enlarged several times. *Author's collection.*

major change to the building, which continues to serve the literary needs of local residents.

The origin of the Upper Sandusky Community Library can be traced to a presentation Reverend Nathaniel Barrett Coulson Love arranged in the mid-1880s. He invited representatives from the Methodist Episcopal Publishing Company to discuss plans for starting a library in Upper Sandusky. Lowell B. Harris attended the talk and offered to match any funds raised. Over $2,000 in money and books were donated. The new Harris Library opened in the basement of the John Stewart Methodist Church. When a new church building was erected in 1899, the library was forced out and found a new home in the Union School.

A small account to erect a permanent library was started by the Usando Literary Club in April 1912. Funds originally were solicited door to door before a request was sent to Andrew Carnegie, who responded favorably. The Carnegie Public Library was completed in 1914 and dedicated on November 19. During its fiftieth anniversary, an addition was added. The expanded building served the community of Upper Sandusky until

1986. Ground was broken for a new library facility in April 1985, and the cornerstone was set that November. All the books, furniture and equipment were moved from the old building to the new building during April 1986. The new Upper Sandusky Community Library opened its doors in April and was formally dedicated on November 28, 1986. It continues to offer educational services to the public and promotes the county's history through the Heritage Room.

Henry Deisel began hand-rolling cigars in 1884 in Lima, Ohio. Two years later, he was joined by Henry and William Demmer, creating the Deisel-Wemmer Company. Their 250 employees could not meet the demand, and an additional plant was opened in Lima. By 1905, the company had expanded into nearby towns to meet the ever-growing desire for its products. Some of the new factories opened by 1913 were in Findlay, Bucyrus, Sidney, Bellefontaine and Toledo. The last two factories to be established by the company were in Upper Sandusky and Sandusky in 1919. At its peak, the company had seventeen factories and employed over 4,000 persons. Cigar-rolling machines were invented in 1915, resulting in much larger production numbers. To take advantage of this new technology and a huge postwar demand, the Deisel-Wemmer Company decided to expand once again.

The new San Felice and El Verso factory began operations on September 24, 1919, in a three-story building located at the corner of Sandusky and Johnson Streets in Upper Sandusky. The name can still be seen painted along the top of the building. A small force of several hundred worked on the second floor. By 1925, demand for cigars had begun to wane, and the company found itself closing and consolidating several plants, including the one at Upper Sandusky. In 1929, the company merged with the Gilbert Cigar Company, creating the Deisel-Wemmer-Gilbert (DWG) Cigar Company, remnants of which still exist today.

Henry Harrison Smith was born on November 28, 1836, in Negrotown in northern Wyandot County and died on October 22, 1922. He is interred in the Smith Mausoleum in the town of Smithville, which was named for his parents. A very prosperous businessman, he decided to give back to the community of Upper Sandusky. In 1921, Smith donated nearly sixteen acres along the south side of today's East Wyandot Avenue to the village for a public park. Shortly afterward, the remaining members of R. Robbins Post No. 91 Grand Army of the Republic convinced the Pennsylvania Railroad to sell them one and a half acres to add to the park. Here they developed a picnic grove and shelter house before donating it to Upper Sandusky in 1926. The area was marked by a large boulder inscribed as a memorial to

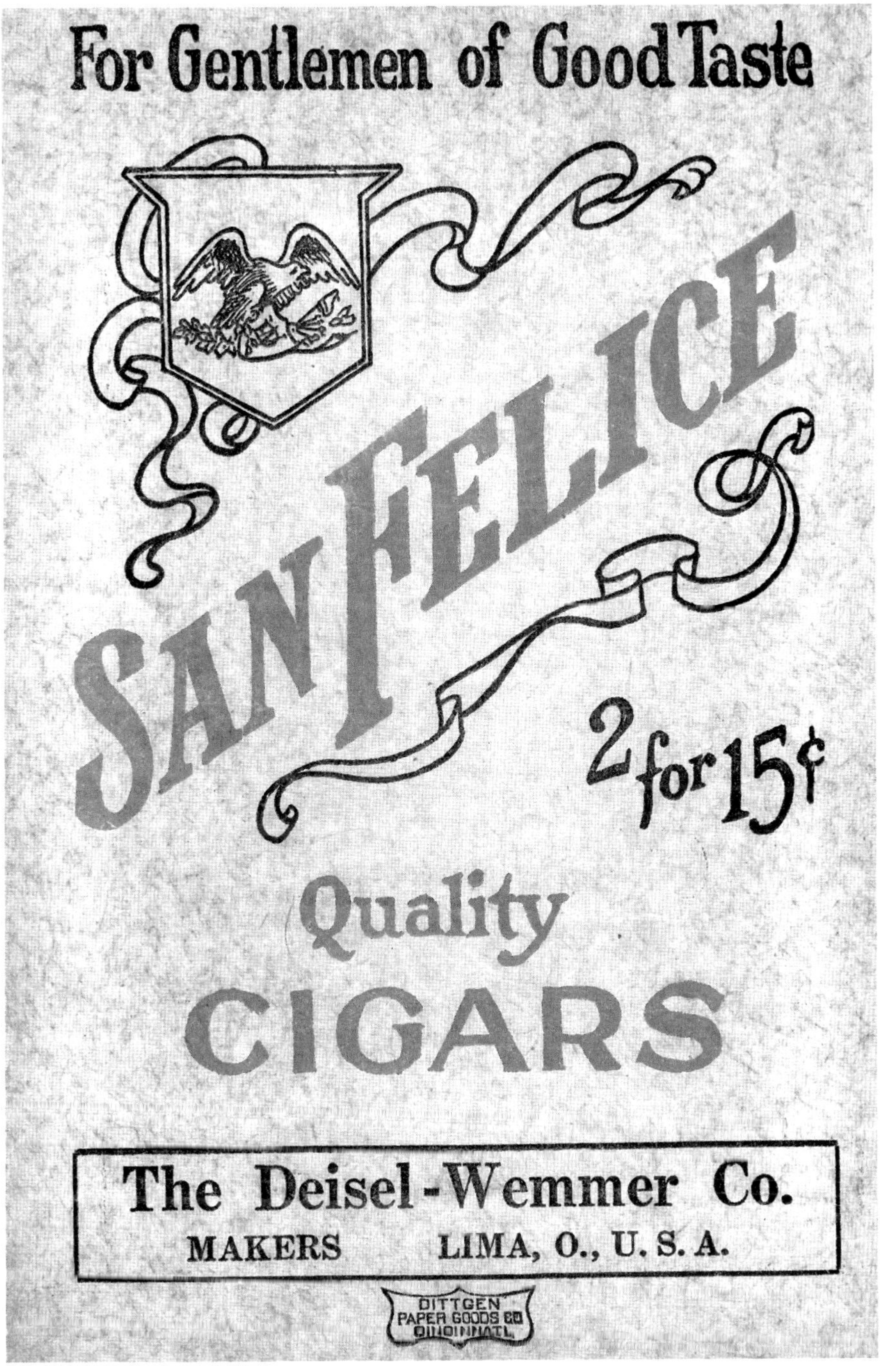

San Felice and El Verso cigars were manufactured at the Upper Sandusky factory in the 1920s and packed in pouches like this one. *Wyandot County Historical Society.*

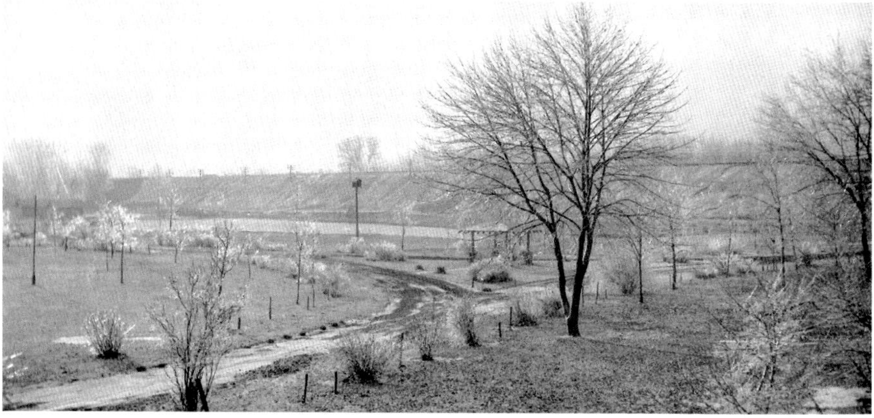

Photograph from the west edge looking roughly southeast across Harrison Smith Park in 1928. The Pennsylvania Railroad tracks run along the south edge. *Wyandot County Historical Society.*

the members of the post. On October 29, 2011, the Wyandot Memorial Association dedicated a new Robbins' Rock Memorial in the park.

Schwilk's Pond was upgraded into a swimming pool for area residents. Two bathhouses were constructed for the pool and now serve as storage sheds. During the mid-1900s, a concrete outdoor swimming pool was constructed, and the old "swimmin' hole" was turned into a fishing pond. Today, the thirty-three-acre Harrison Smith Park features shelter houses, basketball and tennis courts, ball diamonds, playground equipment and an amphitheater for visitors to enjoy. The Park Pond Bridge, a thirty-two-foot-long, Howe truss–inspired covered bridge, was erected in the park in 1972 by members of the Upper Sandusky High School Industrial Arts Club. This is the third bridge to span the small pond of water. One interesting feature, near the rear of the park, is a concrete teepee that marks the execution and burial spot of Soo-de-Nooks, a Wyandotte executed in October 1830 for murdering another in a drunken rage.

One of the best-known stage actresses of the late 1800s and early 1900s was Florence Richmond Boyd, who spent time with her daughter, Nellie Smith, in Wyandot County during her later years. She was born near Kirkpatrick, Marion County, in 1850. At the age of sixteen, Florence taught school before moving to New York City to study elocution. Her teacher, the famous stage actress Fanny Morant, soon introduced her to the theater. Florence specialized in Shakespearian roles, but her biggest hits were the plays *Led Astray* and *East Lynn*. She toured England, Scotland and Ireland,

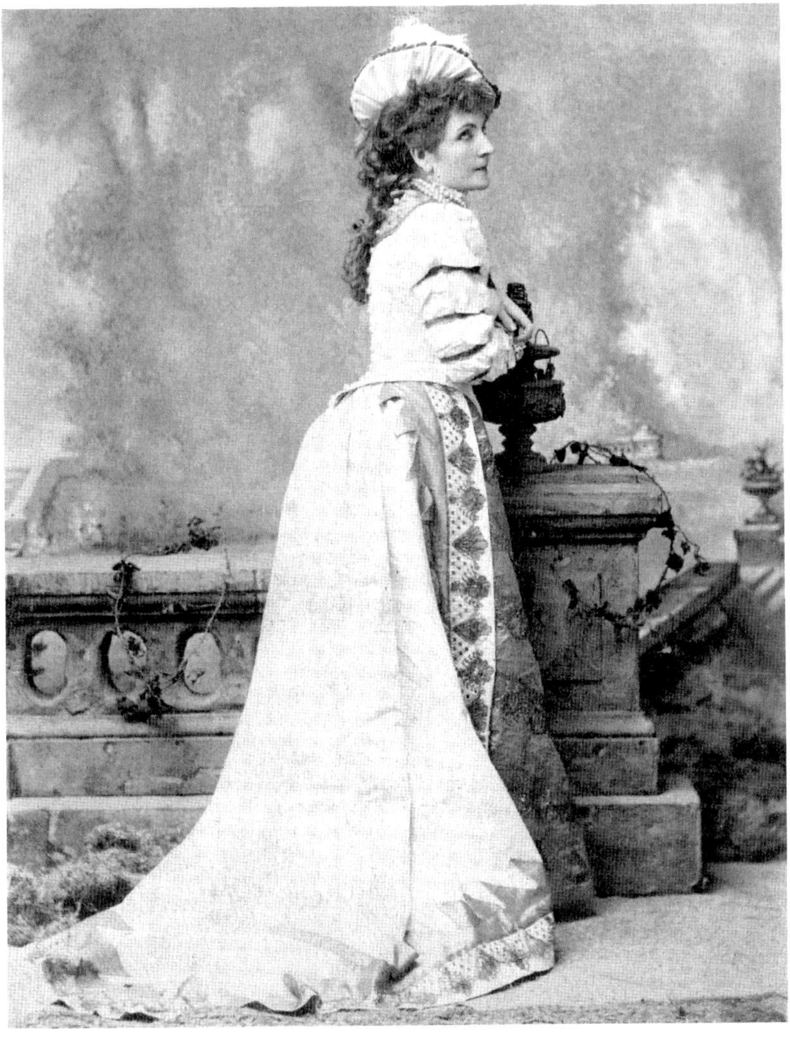

Cabinet card featuring the famous stage actress Florence Richmond Boyd, who is interred in the Boyd Family Mausoleum in Oak Hill Cemetery. *Wyandot County Historical Society.*

where she was most popular. Early in her career, she appeared in *The Hunchback of Notre Dame* at the Opera House in Upper Sandusky.

In 1877, Florence married W. Andrew Boyd, publisher of Boyd directories. The couple had one son and two daughters. Following the birth of her son, Florence retired from the stage, appearing only at charitable benefits, such as the Wyandot County homecoming program. She erected the Boyd mausoleum in Upper Sandusky's Oak Hill Cemetery a few years before her death. Florence died on October 11, 1939, in Tarzana, California, a suburb of Hollywood, and was buried in the family crypt beside her son. Interestingly, two of her pallbearers were the sons of Cyrus Sears, the Medal of Honor recipient.

W. Andrew and Florence Boyd's son, William Stage Boyd, was born on December 18, 1889, in New York City. Like his mother, he began his theatrical career on the stage, appearing on Broadway in *Peter Pan* in 1906. The play *What Price Glory?* was considered his greatest stage performance. He moved to Hollywood in 1913 following the debut of talking pictures. Boyd progressed from taking small roles to starring in motion pictures. A respected character actor, he found instant success appearing in such pictures as *The Locked Door*, *The False Madonna*, *State's Attorney*, *Oliver Twist* and *House on 56th Street.*

In order to differentiate him from the other William Boyd, best known as "Hopalong Cassidy," a California judge gave him his "Stage" moniker. Unfortunately, he had drug and alcohol issues during his career that nearly destroyed both William Boyds' careers, as their images were often mixed up in newspaper accounts. Married and divorced twice, William finally succumbed to ailments related to his alcohol and drug use on March 20, 1935, in Los Angeles, California. He was brought to Wyandot County and interred in the Boyd Family Mausoleum in Oak Hill Cemetery.

7

Growth and Prosperity

As the twentieth century progressed, Wyandot County residents aspired to the amenities afforded to larger cities and counties throughout the United States. Improvements could be seen springing up across the county, from an expanded highway system to an airport and modern hospital. Veterans returning from overseas used their newfound abilities and expertise to start new businesses and positively impact the lives of their fellow residents.

A small group of interested persons met on May 17, 1938, to discuss the need for a public library in Sycamore. The next month, a small library opened in an upstairs room on Main Street. For the next eight years, the Sycamore Library operated as a branch of the Upper Sandusky Community Library. In 1947, it became known as the Sycamore School District Library and moved to a downstairs room on West Seventh Street in 1951.

Seven years later, Alice Vance donated land on East Seventh Street in Sycamore for the construction of a new library building, which was dedicated in 1960. The library continued to operate until August 26, 1984, when a building project was dedicated, doubling its size. Recognizing its regional patronage, in 1986, the name was changed to the Mohawk Community Library. Outgrowing itself in the late 1990s, the building was expanded, once again doubling its size. The current library was dedicated on June 14, 1998. Another expansion, housing a new meeting room, was dedicated on December 8, 2013. The library continues to serve the literary needs of the local area.

During the late 1940s, residents of four townships (Salem, Pitt, Crane and Mifflin) saw the need for a modern hospital in Wyandot County. After initial

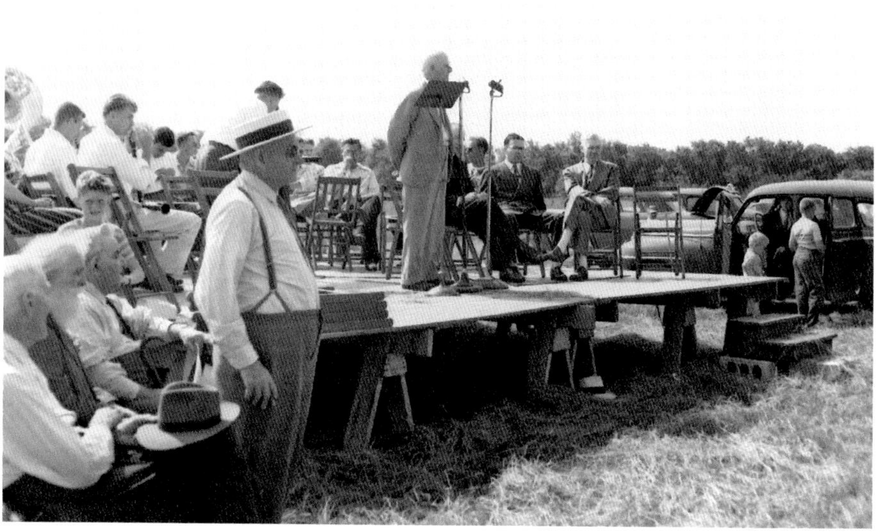

Speakers and guests sit on the makeshift stage at the Wyandot Memorial Hospital groundbreaking ceremony in June 1949. The building was completed the following year. *Wyandot County Historical Society.*

planning by a committee representing the townships, a groundbreaking ceremony for the new Wyandot Memorial Hospital was held on June 20, 1949, in front of several hundred persons. Adam F. Gamber, president of the Joint Township Hospital Board of Trustees, turned over the first shovelful of dirt in a plot north of Upper Sandusky beside the fairgrounds. The formal program featured Father William J. McKeown, the Jenny Lind Trio and Judge Russell H. Kear.

The funding for the building came from three distinct sources: 1) a bond issue to raise funds, 2) financial aid secured from governmental agencies and 3) nearly three thousand local donors. The F.M. Vaughn Building Company of Hamilton, Ohio, was awarded the contract to erect the hospital and began foundation excavations shortly after the ceremony ended. Construction took place over the next year with R.P. McGill overseeing the project.

The $400,000 hospital was officially dedicated on September 11, 1950, with roughly three thousand spectators in attendance. A representative of the construction company presented the hospital keys to Adam Gamber. Fred J. Milligan, a Columbus attorney with ties to the county, and Dr. Anthony J. Borowsky, chief of the office of Hospital Facilities State Department of Health, were the featured speakers. Following the ceremony, the attendees were given the opportunity to tour the new facility.

The Wyandot Memorial Hospital opened to the public as a nonprofit facility governed by a joint Township Board of Trustees. It offered routine medical, surgical and maternity services to local residents. Between October 2010 and the spring of 2012, the hospital leaders engaged in a construction program that enlarged the building and expanded the Emergency Department. According to the hospital website, it features sixteen medical and surgical beds, five intensive care beds and four maternity beds. The Wyandot Health Foundation Inc., a tax-exempt organization, was established on June 10, 1985, to raise funds for the Wyandot Memorial Hospital. Located in Upper Sandusky, it remains the only hospital in the county.

In the early 1950s, residents discussed the possibility of constructing an airport. The County Airport Authority was established and began overseeing the project. On September 1, 1955, the new airport was opened to the public. It consists of a single asphalt-and-concrete runway measuring roughly four thousand feet long by seventy-five feet wide. Situated northwest of Upper Sandusky, the airport complex covers a little more than one hundred acres.

The most famous murder case in Wyandot County history was the "Red Slipper Murder," which occurred in 1953. Although the actual murder took place in Delaware County, it was detectives from the Wyandot County Sheriff's Office who solved the case.

The story begins with a young lady leaving her home in White Plains, New York, to attend Ohio Wesleyan University in Delaware, Ohio. Cynthia Anne Pfeil soon met and began a relationship with Roy R. Schinagle Jr. of Mayfield Heights, Ohio, a relationship of which reportedly her parents did not approve. She returned home to New York after her freshman year at college, took a job in Cleveland and then snuck down to Delaware to see her boyfriend in September 1953. The couple met at a small shack near the campus where he told her to stay while he was out.

A few days later, on September 18, a woman's body was discovered along a roadside in northern Wyandot County. She was clad in just a flannel nightgown and red slippers. Her face was mangled, making recognition virtually impossible. A local funeral home worked on her face so that a picture could be placed in local newspapers in the hopes that someone might recognize her. Without much luck, Sheriff Dean McAllister focused on the only physical evidence left at the scene. His investigators learned that the red slippers were made by a cobbler shop in Columbus, Ohio, and shipped to White Plains. Upon visiting the town, they were introduced to the mother of Cynthia Pfeil, who had not heard from her daughter recently. The men traveled to Ohio Wesleyan, where they interviewed several of Cynthia's

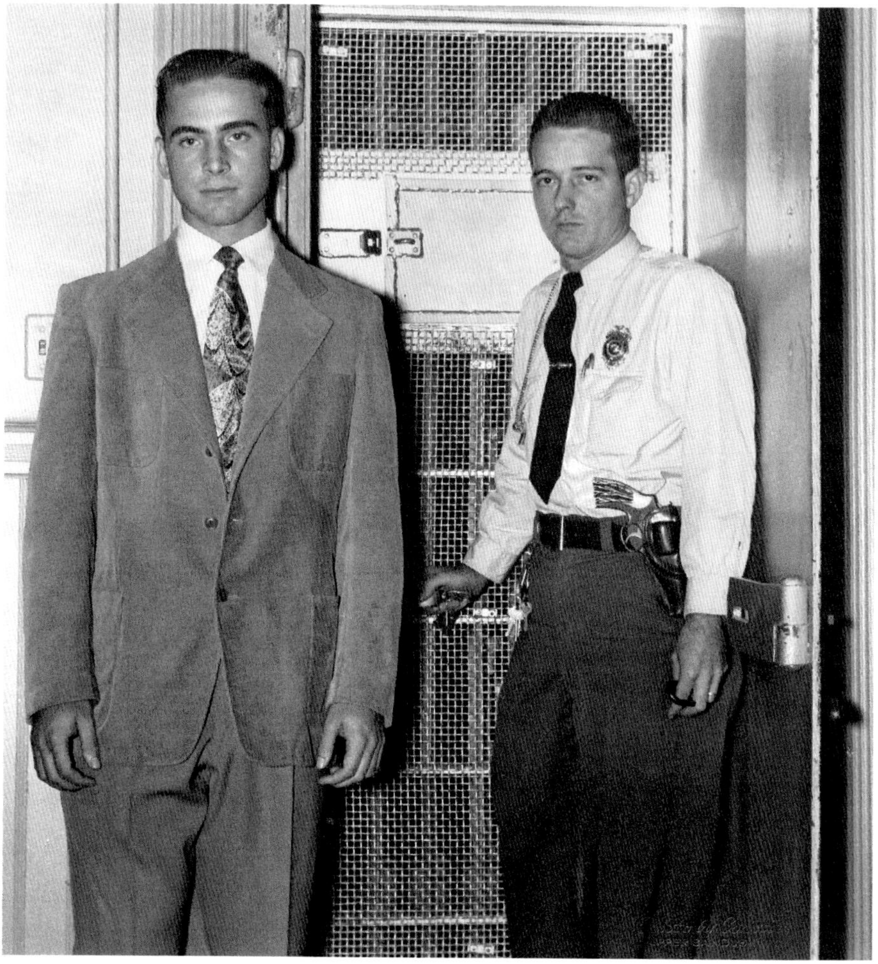

Roy Schinagle and Sheriff Dean McCallister pose following Schinagle's confession to killing Cynthia Pfiel in the infamous Red Slipper Murder case. *Wyandot County Historical Society.*

friends and learned of numerous arguments between the couple, making Roy the prime suspect.

Roy Schinagle was soon arrested and brought in for questioning by Sheriff McAllister. On September 24, he signed a nine-page typed confession regarding the murder. He told investigators that Cynthia had left the shack against his wishes and had been spotted. He then went in a blind rage, striking and choking Cynthia until she died. He supposedly panicked and tried to revive her. When that didn't work he struck her face multiple times with a metal pipe to disfigure her, placed her in his trunk and drove north for a couple of hours before dumping her body near a small clump of woods. After his admission, he led Delaware police to the location of the pipe.

Cynthia, only nineteen years old and pregnant at the time, was buried at Calvary Cemetery in White Plains on September 25. Schinagle was indicted on charges of first-degree murder by the Wyandot County Grand Jury. His life was spared by her parents in October when they agreed to let him plead guilty to second-degree murder in exchange for life in prison. He was paroled in 1963 after serving only ten years in prison. He returned to northeast Ohio, where he has lived as a free man ever since, despite somewhat hiding his past.

One of the most tragic and least known incidents in Wyandot County history occurred on the night of March 5, 1967. Lake Central Airlines Flight 527 crashed about three miles southeast of Marseilles, killing all thirty-eight persons onboard (three crew and thirty-five passengers). A Convair CV-580 propeller plane (N73130), operated by Lake Central Airlines, departed Columbus, Ohio, at 7:52 p.m. bound for Toledo. At 8:07 p.m., all four blades on the right side engine separated from the propeller. The number-two blade penetrated the fuselage, forcing the plane to crash into snow-covered farm fields along County Highway 94. It left a debris trail about one and a half miles long through Wyandot, Hardin and Marion Counties. According to newspaper and official reports, the plane came down "flat" and broke into two major pieces without exploding on impact. Many of the victims were found still belted in their seats.

Following the crash, the remains of the victims were moved to a temporary morgue set up in the then-vacant Mifflin High School, where they were identified and released to family members. This was the first crash of a Convair CV-580 airplane in the United States and is the second-worst death toll for this type of aircraft in the world. Ohio Aviation director Norman Crabtree noted at the time that this was the first crash of a scheduled airliner in Ohio "as far back as he could remember." The National Transportation Safety Board concluded that the crash was a result of "the failure of the right propeller due to the omission of the torque piston nitriding (hardening) process during manufacture, and the failure of manufacturing quality control to detect the omission." A direct result of this disaster was the inspection of all aircraft using similar engines. Several additional "soft" piston O-rings were discovered in other airliners and replaced before any further lives were lost.

One of Wyandot County's most famous residents lived in the area for only a few years during the early 1940s. Neil A. Armstrong, the first man on the moon, was born on a farm outside Wapakoneta on August 5, 1930. His father, Stephen, worked for the State of Ohio Auditor's Office and was stationed throughout northwestern Ohio. Between 1941 and 1944, the Armstrong family lived in the house at 464 North Sandusky Avenue in Upper Sandusky.

While here, Neil was an active member of Boy Scout Troop No. 25 and spent a lot of time hanging out in Harrison Smith Park. Former classmates recall that his love of aeronautics began at an early age. In fact, he obtained his pilot's license before his driver's license. In an interview during his later years, Neil once mentioned that his first job was mowing grass at the Mission Church Cemetery while he was only ten years old. He earned a whopping ten cents an hour. Later, he worked for Neumeister's Bakery in Upper Sandusky cleaning the bread mixer.

Neil attended the Upper Sandusky Junior High School, playing baritone horn in the school band under the direction of C.W. Assenheimer. His freshman year, he attended the Upper Sandusky High School and founded a jazz combo known as the "Mississippi Moonshiners."

The Armstrong family worshiped at Upper Sandusky's Trinity Evangelical and Reformed Church, now known as Trinity United Church of Christ, where Neil was confirmed on June 13, 1943. Following his time in Upper Sandusky, Neil moved with his family to Wapakoneta, the town with which he is most associated. On July 20, 1969, he became the first person to set foot on the moon as part of the Apollo 11 mission. Neil Armstrong passed away on August 25, 2012, but will always be remembered as an American hero.

One of the more recent events that generated much excitement in the county during the summer of 1993 was the filming of scenes in Upper Sandusky for the upcoming film *The Shawshank Redemption*. Two primary locations were selected: the Wyandot County Courthouse and the former Stevens Lumber Company building. The restored third-floor courtroom was featured in early scenes regarding the trial of Andy Dufresne, portrayed by Tim Robbins. Several local residents served as extras during the court scenes.

Scenes of the prison woodworking shop were shot in the old Stevens Lumber Company woodshop. Many of the original woodworking machines were brought back temporarily by owner Bill Mullen to bring the building to life. Mullen also helped round up numerous 1930s and 1940s vintage vehicles for use in the movie. Several locals portrayed inmates in the scenes. Tim Robbins and Morgan Freeman, who portrayed Red, filmed scenes in the town and could be observed walking the streets of Upper Sandusky between filming sessions.

Several reunions of the extras have taken place over the ensuing years, often raising funds for community projects, such as the restoration of *Lady Justice*. Bill and April Mullins opened a small Shawshank Museum in the

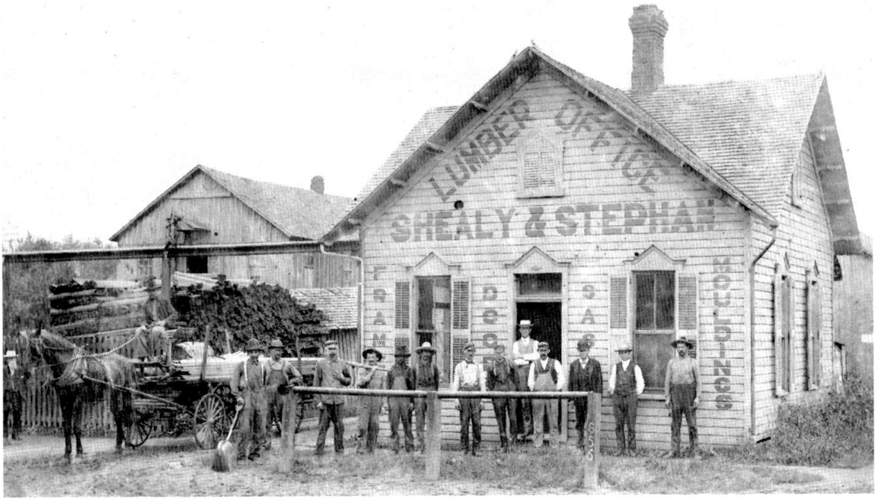

Original Shealy and Stephan Lumber Company building. The later brick Stephan Lumber building was featured as the woodshop in *The Shawshank Redemption*. *Wyandot County Historical Society*.

Stevens Lumber Company building. Occasionally, actors from the film return to Upper Sandusky to greet the diehard fans of the acclaimed movie.

Sydne Rome was born on March 17, 1951, in Akron, Ohio, and lived with her family in Upper Sandusky until age eighteen, when she moved to Europe to pursue a film career. In 1969, she made her debut in the British comedy *Some Girls Do*. Although most of her films would be considered risqué for the time, she did appear alongside the likes of Roger Moore, Susannah York, Jodie Foster and Shelly Winters and starred in the movie *What?* directed by Roman Polanski. During the fitness craze of the 1980s, she became well known for her fitness videos, rivalling Jane Fonda. Rome was also a professional singer, having success in Germany, Spain and Italy. She currently lives in Italy with her second husband.

The Lincoln Highway was the first route to follow the corridor of U.S. Route 30 through Ohio. As noted in an earlier chapter, the route was established in 1913. Its path changed multiple times as the highway adjusted to include recently paved sections of road throughout the state and county. In 1928, the route was formally designated as Inter-County Highway 200 and known by locals as the Bucyrus-Upper Sandusky Road. Finally, in 1939, the Lincoln Highway realignment project was completed, and the highway became the modern U.S. 30 corridor. At the time, the section of road between the Indiana state line and Mansfield was known as State Route

5, including roughly nineteen miles in Wyandot County. By the 1960s, it had received the U.S. Route 30-N signs, designating the highway between Mansfield and Delphos. The final name and signage for U.S. 30 through western Ohio occurred in November 1973.

As traffic along the U.S. 30 corridor expanded beyond its safe capacity in the late 1980s, the state embarked on a plan to expand all 250 miles of the roadway into a four-lane highway. Plans for the western Ohio section were constantly getting delayed until 1990, when the Ohio Department of Transportation (ODOT) committed to improving the section between Beaverdam and Bucyrus. On March 2, 1992, the state began construction of the highway bypass around Upper Sandusky. This new stretch of road around the north side of Upper Sandusky opened to the public on June 21, 1994 and ran concurrent with U.S. Route 23.

Groundbreaking for the new four-lane U.S. 30 upgrade from Upper Sandusky to Bucyrus took place in July 2001. The $75 million, eleven-mile highway began construction in August 2001 and opened to the public on December 14, 2004. The remaining section of U.S. 30 in western Wyandot County from State Route 235 to the U.S. 23 bypass near Upper Sandusky officially began on May 13, 2005, when a groundbreaking ceremony was held for the project. The $98.8 million, twenty-six-mile four-lane highway officially opened to vehicular traffic on November 9, 2007.

In 1961, the Ohio Department of Transportation announced plans to relocate and expand the route of United States Route 23 from Carey to Delaware. Between October 12, 1962, and October 1964, construction of a four-lane U.S. 23 was completed from Findlay to State Route 182 south of Upper Sandusky. Over the next year, the rest of the highway bypass from Ohio 182 back to the original alignment of U.S. 23 was completed. In 1967, the highway from Upper Sandusky to the Wyandot County line was expanded. Initial plans were announced in 1991 by ODOT for the current U.S. Route 30 bypass around Upper Sandusky.

The Lincoln Historic Byway, officially designated in March 2004, follows the original 240-mile alignment of the 1928 route, primarily the current U.S. Route 30 through Ohio. In addition to Wyandot County, the byway runs through the counties of Allen, Ashland, Columbiana, Crawford, Hancock, Richland, Stark, Van Wert and Wayne. In 2001, the Ohio Historical Society, in conjunction with the Ohio Lincoln Highway League, erected a historical marker honoring the highway along East Wyandot Avenue in Upper Sandusky. Near the marker is a small brick segment of the old Lincoln Highway alignment. When the Red Bridge was removed and replaced with the George Washington Bridge in the 1930s, the route was straightened, leaving a brick remnant behind Willson's Grocery that can still be traveled.

Taking a look into the future and recognizing the need for renewable energy, Wyandot County decided to invest in solar energy while other counties were constructing wind turbines. On August 19, 2010, Governor

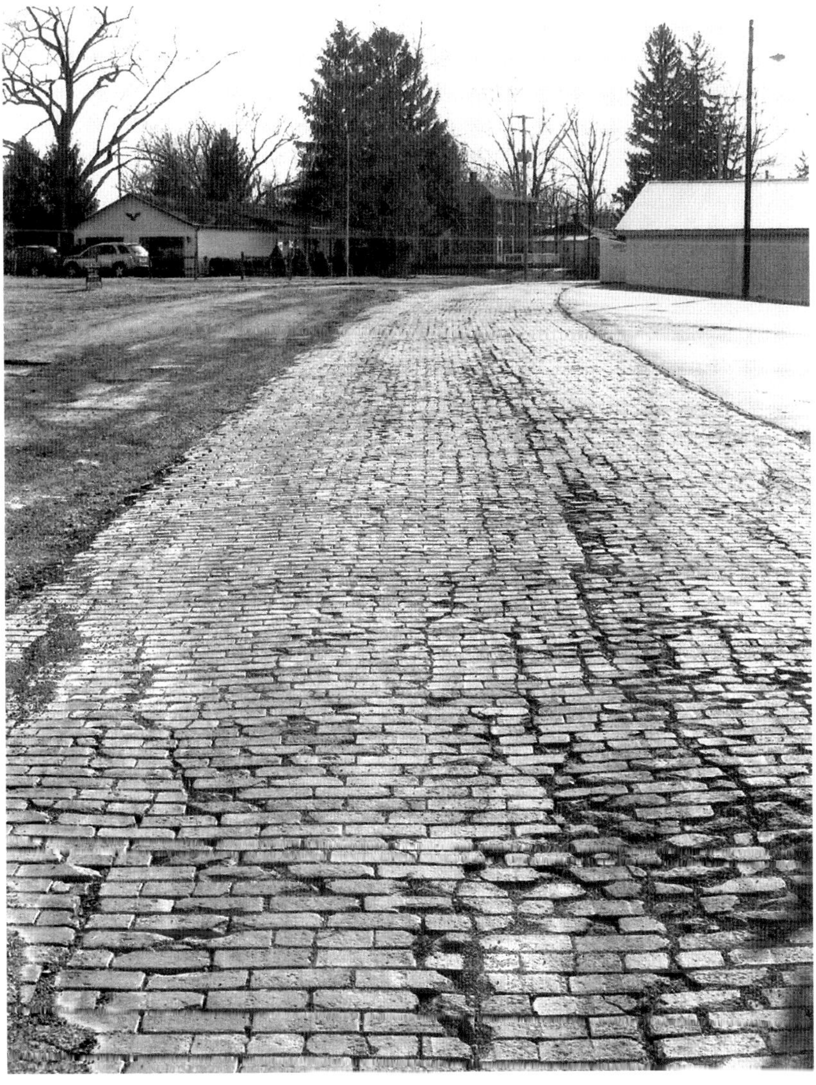

Remnant of the Lincoln Highway behind Willson's Grocery in Upper Sandusky. This was left over from the realignment of the route in the 1930s. *Author's collection.*

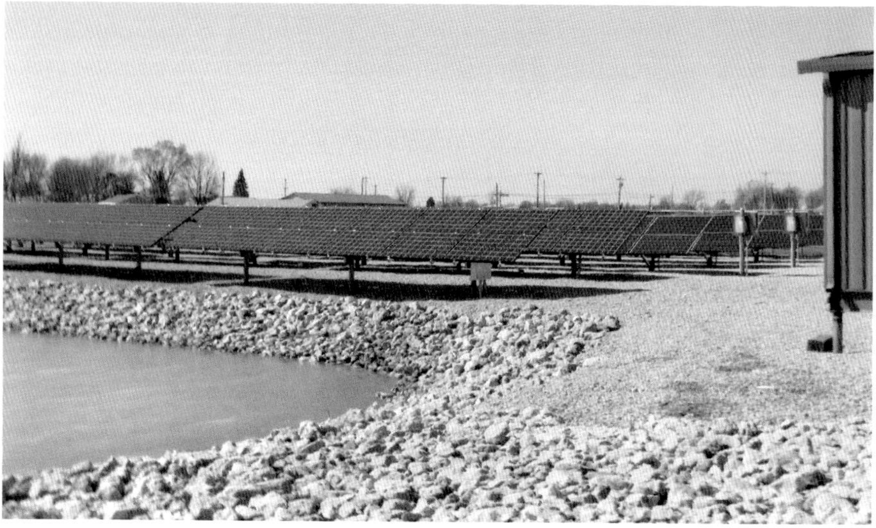

A close-up view of the solar panel array located next to Vaughn Industries of Carey, a leader in renewable energy resources in the region. *Author's collection.*

Ted Strickland dedicated the 83.9-acre Wyandot Solar Farm, situated beside the Wyandot County Airport north of Upper Sandusky. Operated by the Public Service Enterprise Group, the 159,200 ground-mounted solar panels produce twelve megawatts of electricity, producing power for over nine thousand homes. At the time of its dedication, it was the largest solar installation operating in Ohio. Construction began on October 22, 2009, by Vaughn Industries of Carey and was completed in April 2010. On December 29, 2014, the Carey Solar Farm went online. The two megawatt–generating farm sits just outside Carey and provides power to the city. The $8 million project was built by Vaughn Industries.

During my research, I uncovered some additional interesting twentieth-century historical items and hereby share with the reader. The Dorsey Brothers Orchestra recorded the song "Dusk in Upper Sandusky," which was released under the Jimmy Dorsey label in 1948. Carl N. Karcher was born near Upper Sandusky in 1917 and founded the hamburger chain Carl's Jr. in 1954. The parents of Dr. Sam Shepherd, the inspiration for the 1960s television show *The Fugitive* lived in Upper Sandusky at one time. Ralph Schuler operated a blacksmith shop in the county until 1963 and, at one time, worked on the sculptures at Mount Rushmore. Aliens invaded Upper Sandusky in 1986, at least according to video game creator Steve Meretzky's release "Leather Goddesses of Phobos."

8

A Tradition of Military Service

Men and women from Wyandot County have served in the U.S. Armed Forces in every major conflict from the American Revolution to the most recent conflicts in Iraq and Afghanistan. Even before the county was settled, its future residents were taking part in conflicts that would eventually shape the nation. Veterans from the American Revolution, the French and Indian War and the War of 1812 later settled in the region and rest in its local cemeteries.

During three of the major conflicts fought after the establishment of the county, naval vessels named in honor of the Wyandotte Nation helped to support the soldiers on land and protect the entire United States. Most local residents have heard of the USS *Wyandot*, constructed during World War II and named for Wyandot County, but not many are aware of the two other naval ships that were renamed the USS *Wyandotte* during the American Civil War and the Spanish-American War.

The USS *Wyandotte* was a merchant steamer built at Philadelphia in 1853 as the USS *Western Port*. The ship was chartered by the Department of the Navy in 1858 to participate in an American naval expedition to Asunción, Paraguay. After the vessel had been fitted out as a gunboat, the USS *Western Port* was commissioned by the U.S. Navy on October 27, 1858. Following successful negotiations, the ship returned to the United States and was decommissioned on May 28, 1859. It was purchased by the Department of the Navy on June 6, 1859, and renamed the USS *Wyandotte* in honor of the Wyandotte Indians.

After repairs, the ship was recommissioned on September 19, 1859. It spent much of the next year patrolling the Atlantic Ocean and the Caribbean suppressing the slave trade. On May 9, 1860, it captured off the coast of Cuba the *William*, a slave ship carrying 570 Africans.

Early in the Civil War, the ship protected federal military installations along the Gulf coast. In late 1860 and early 1861, it protected Florida's coastal forts and preserved Key West for the Union. In May 1861, the ship aided in the naval blockade of the Confederate States of America. Following severe damage, the ship sailed to the New York Navy Yard on August 23, 1861, for major repairs. It was then dispatched for additional blockade duties in South Carolina, Georgia and Florida until returning to New York for additional repairs on July 25, 1862.

The ship left the naval yard for duties as a guard vessel on September 1. It served in the Potomac River and Hampton Roads, Virginia. On April 11, 1863, the ship resumed blockade duty. However, due to all the previous damage, it could no longer handle rough seas and was declared unfit for guard duty only on October 3, 1863. The ship spent the remainder of the war off the coast of Virginia.

The USS *Wyandotte* was decommissioned at the New York Navy Yard on June 3, 1865, and was sold on July 12, 1865. The ship was returned to merchant service on September 23, 1865, but ran aground near Duxbury, Massachusetts, on January 26, 1866. It was later declared damaged beyond economical repair and scrapped.

The USS *Wyandotte* was a Canonicus-class monitor ship originally named the USS *Tippecanoe*. It was constructed by Miles Greenwood at the shipyard of John Litherbury in Cincinnati. The USS *Tippecanoe* was laid down on September 28, 1862; commissioned on April 16, 1864; and launched on December 22, 1864. The warship was not completed until 1866, when it was laid up at New Orleans, Louisiana, for additional armaments.

In 1869, the ship was twice renamed: the USS *Vesuvius* on June 15 and the USS *Wyandotte* on August 10. In 1873 and 1874, the ship underwent extensive repairs and overhauling by John Roach & Sons at Chester, Pennsylvania. On January 24, 1876, the warship was recommissioned by the U.S. Navy. It was based out of Hampton Roads, Virginia, and later in Washington, D.C., until being deactivated in 1885. The USS *Wyandotte* was transferred from the navy to the Connecticut State Militia in 1896.

At the beginning of the Spanish-American War, many eastern coastal cities were nervous about a Spanish attack. In response, the navy reactivated several Civil War–era ships, including the USS *Wyandotte*, to protect these port cities. On April 30, 1898, the ship was recommissioned and sailed from New Haven, Connecticut, to guard Boston, Massachusetts, where it was stationed from May 19 to September 5. After the war ended, the ship traveled to Philadelphia, where it was decommissioned on September 20, 1898. The ship was sold for scrap on January 17, 1899.

The USS *Wyandot* (AKA-92) was an Andromeda-class attack cargo ship officially named after Wyandot County, Ohio. The ship was laid down on May 6, 1944, by the Moore Dry Dock Company of Oakland, California. It was launched on June 28 and acquired by the Department of the Navy and commissioned on September 30. Following a shakedown cruise, it departed San Francisco on November 25 bound for the Hawaiian Islands. The ship departed Pearl Harbor on January 26, 1945, and proceeded to the Philippines. There it joined in the assault on Okinawa, Japan, receiving a battle star for its actions.

Following the end of World War II, the USS *Wyandot* operated out of Norfolk, Virginia. It participated in exercises throughout the Atlantic Ocean and Caribbean, Artic and Mediterranean Seas. From 1955 to 1958, the ship

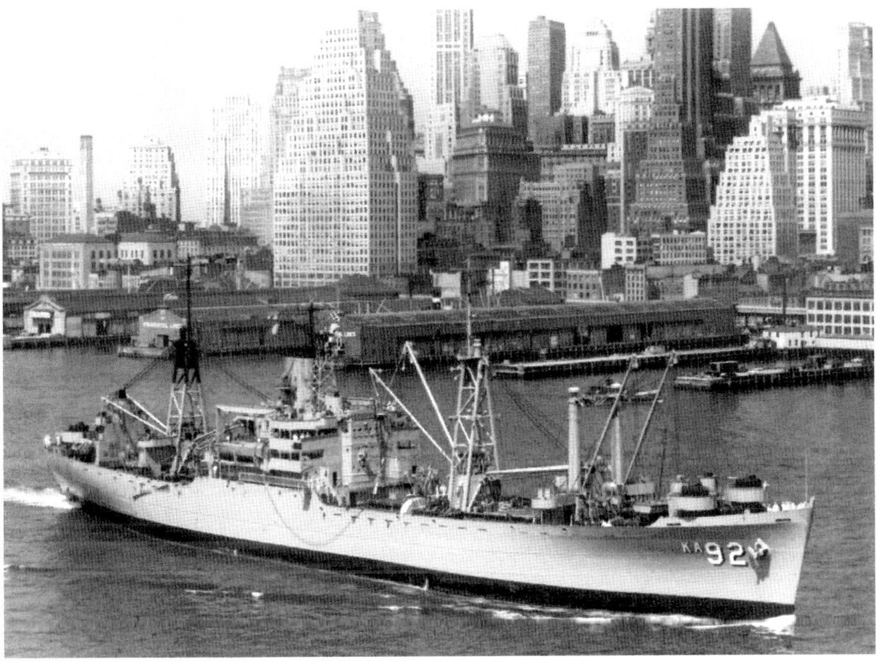

The USS *Wyandot*, an Andromeda-class attack cargo ship constructed during World War II, later served during Operation Deep Freeze in Antarctica. *Wyandot County Historical Society*.

took part in Operations Deep Freeze I, II, III and IV, eventually helping to establish Ellsworth Station in Antarctica.

The USS *Wyandot* was decommissioned on July 10, 1959, and struck from the navy rolls. However, on July 1, 1960, the ship was reinstated due to tensions in Berlin, Germany. It was transferred as T-AKA-92 to the Military Sea Transportation Service in March 1963. Later reclassified as T-AK-283, the ship was transferred to the Military Sealift Command. On October 31, 1975, the ship was placed in the U.S. Maritime Administration Reserve Fleet. Ironically, the USS *Wyandot* was sold for scrap to Japan's Nissho Iwai Corporation on November 5, 1987. A photograph of the ship is located just inside the entrance of the Wyandot County Courthouse.

Even before Wyandot County was formally established, its future residents were serving in military units throughout the world in addition to those of the United States. Johann Peter Binau was born on April 27, 1799, in Hessen-Darmstadt, Germany. He married Anna Barbara Marquardt, and the couple had nine children. He and his wife, with their children, immigrated to America in 1847. The family arrived in New York in September and made their way toward their new homestead outside of Carey. John, as he was known in Ohio, died on June 25, 1879, in Salem Township and was buried in the Salem Lutheran Church Cemetery.

Johann was one of the personal bodyguards of Louis I, the Grand Duke of Hessia, for nearly five years. He served in the Second Battalion, Company Captain Schultz and was discharged from military service on April 1, 1826, at Darmstadt, Germany, after a little over six years and nine months. As a memento for his faithful service, Binau was given an ornamental sword, which he brought with him to Wyandot County in 1847. The sword was placed in the family cabin and remained there until the 1920s. It subsequently passed through the family until October 16, 2012, when the sword was donated by his descendants to the Wyandot County Museum.

James Alexander White is one of the least-known veterans buried in Wyandot County, yet the story of one of his earliest battles is perhaps the most famous in the world. Of the 625 soldiers who participated, he was 1 of only 26 men to survive the infamous "Charge of the Light Brigade" at Balaclava during the Crimean War, which was fought between Great Britain and Russia during the early 1850s.

Born in County Ayer, Scotland, in August 1821, James first immigrated to America in the late 1840s. When Great Britain declared war, he returned to England and enlisted in the military. He was assigned to the Light Brigade of British Cavalry under the command of James Thomas Brudenell, better known as Lord Cardigan. It was in this unit that he participated in the failed charge on October 25, 1854. White participated in seven battles during the war and was injured only once, nearly dying from a blow to the head during the yearlong Battle of Sebastopol.

Following the war, he returned to America, eventually settling in Pitt Township, Wyandot County, in 1857. When the American Civil War broke out, White enlisted three separate times with the Union army. On April 20, 1861, he enlisted as a private for three months with Captain William T. Wilson's Company C, 15th Regiment, Ohio Volunteer Infantry. Following his discharge in August 1861, he joined a regiment of the Pennsylvania Volunteer Infantry for two years and four months. Finally, he enlisted again as a private on May 2, 1864, in Company G, 144th Regiment, Ohio Volunteer Infantry, serving until being mustered out on August 31, 1864. Amazingly, with all his service during the Civil War, White was never wounded.

According to his obituary, despite his extensive service, he was very reluctant to speak of his military exploits. James married Mary J. Brown, and the couple had four children. White died on September 15, 1900, in Upper Sandusky and was buried beside his wife in Hendrickson Cemetery near Marseilles.

The first conflict following the establishment of Wyandot County was the Mexican War (1845–46), in which numerous local men participated. Roughly one hundred men volunteered in May 1846 to join the "Sandusky Rangers" commanded by Captain John Caldwell. The soldiers were marched from Upper Sandusky to Cincinnati's Camp Washington, where they stayed until being mustered out on June 19. Several of the men subsequently enlisted in other units. A second group of volunteers was organized on June 1, 1846, but for unknown reasons, these men were not accepted for military service.

Captain Caldwell eventually was named the commissary of another active regiment of Ohio volunteers and went to Mexico in 1846. Following the end of the brief conflict, he and the rest of the Wyandot County volunteers returned home from Mexico in June 1847.

The next major conflict was the American Civil War (1861–65). Not expecting the conflict to last long, President Abraham Lincoln requested seventy-five thousand three-month volunteers to fill the ranks of the Union army on May 6, 1861. Wyandot County men once again volunteered for service. The Fifteenth Regiment, Ohio Volunteer Infantry, was among the first to answer the call. Three companies of "one hundred days" men were raised locally by Captain William T. Wilson (Company C), Captain Peter

A. Tyler (Company G) and Captain Isaac M. Kirby (Company I). The companies were discharged on August 31, 1861.

It soon became obvious that this was not going to be a quick conflict, so Wilson, then a lieutenant colonel, began the process of organizing a three-year regiment. The Fifteenth Regiment, Ohio Volunteer Infantry, was mustered at Camp Jackson in Columbus with Captain Kirby in command of Company D, known as the "Warpole Guards," which was composed of Wyandot County men. The soldiers served throughout the South, participating in numerous campaigns. One of the first units to enlist and among the last to be mustered out, the weary troops were finally discharged on December 27, 1865.

The Forty-ninth Regiment, Ohio Volunteer Infantry, included numerous men from Wyandot County, almost entirely comprising Company D. It was organized on September 5, 1861, at Camp Noble near Tiffin, participated in the famed Battle of Chickamauga and served until November 30, 1865.

The Eighty-first Regiment, Ohio Volunteer Infantry, was recruited in the summer of 1861. Captain Peter Tyler commanded Company D, composed almost entirely of Wyandot County men. The soldiers marched out of Benton Barracks on September 24, 1861, and served in the area of Missouri and Kentucky until being discharged on July 21, 1865.

The 101st Regiment, Ohio Volunteer Infantry, was organized in northwest Ohio in 1862. The soldiers were mustered into service at Monroeville, Ohio, on August 30, 1862, including Captain Isaac Kirby's Company F composed of Wyandot County men. On May 3, 1864, the regiment marched with General Sherman on his famed Atlanta Campaign. The men were constantly marching and fighting until being discharged on June 12, 1865, in Alabama.

The 123rd Regiment, Ohio Volunteer Infantry, was recruited from counties in northwest Ohio and organized at Monroeville, Ohio, on September 24, 1862. Men from Wyandot County comprised Companies A and F. On June 13, 1863, the entire regiment surrendered and was soon transported to Libby Prison in Richmond, Virginia. Several of the men were exchanged and attended the surrender at Appomattox Court House. The regiment was mustered out at Camp Chase on June 12 and 13, 1865, and the men began making their way back home.

The 144th Regiment, Ohio National Guard, was organized as a "one hundred days" unit on May 11, 1864, from members of Wyandot County's 19th Battalion and Wood County's 64th Battalion, Ohio National Guard. The regiment suffered some of the heaviest casualties recorded for a local unit, losing nearly 125 men, many of whom died at Andersonville and other Confederate prison camps. Finally on August 31, 1864, the men were mustered out and returned home.

There are numerous veterans—many more than can be addressed in this short chapter—who contributed mightily to the nation's cause during the war and, upon returning home, served their communities well. A Civil War general and two Medal of Honor recipients are among the many men recognized from the conflict with ties to the county. Several soldiers gave their lives and were memorialized as namesakes for local Grand Army of the Republic posts.

Brevet Brigadier General Isaac Minor Kirby was born on February 10, 1835, in Columbus, Ohio. At the beginning of the Civil War, he recruited a group of volunteers and was named captain of Company I, 15th Regiment, Ohio Volunteer Infantry. On August 31, 1861, the unit was mustered out, so he returned home, where he recruited Wyandot County men for a three-year enlistment. He was commissioned captain of Company D in the new 15th Regiment and served until poor health led him to resign his commission on May 4, 1862. In July, he was asked to reenlist to the military and was commissioned a captain in the 101st Regiment, Ohio Volunteer Infantry, and was promoted to major on October 14, 1862.

Due to the deaths of his superior officers at the Battle of Stones River, Tennessee, Kirby was promoted to colonel on January 27, 1863, retroactive to December 26, 1862. Colonel Kirby led the 101st until being named commander of the 1st Brigade, 1st Division, 4th Army Corps, during the Atlanta Campaign in 1864. Following the Battles of Franklin, Tennessee, and Nashville, Tennessee, Kirby received a commission as brevet brigadier general "for meritorious service rendered throughout the war." He remained in command of the brigade until being mustered out with the 101st Regiment on June 12, 1865. He returned to Upper Sandusky and engaged in the mercantile trade, specializing in hardware. Active in politics and veterans' affairs, General Kirby died on May 30, 1917, and was buried in Oak Hill Cemetery.

Cyrus Sears was born on March 10, 1832, in Delaware County, New York. In 1836, he moved with his parents to a farm near Bucyrus, Crawford County, where he lived until 1852. He began the study of law with his brother in 1855, eventually attending Cincinnati Law School. In 1861, he began his law practice in Wyandot County but quickly abandoned it, moved to Cincinnati and joined the Burnet Rifle Company. During July 1861, he began recruiting men to serve in the Eleventh Ohio Independent Battery. When the group was mustered in on August 12, Sears joined as a private.

On October 12, 1861, he was commissioned a first lieutenant in the Eleventh Battery, Ohio Light Artillery. The unit fought in several battles in the South but is best known for the Battle of Iuka, Mississippi, on September 19, 1862. For his actions during the conflict, Sears was awarded the Medal of Honor on December 31, 1892. The official government citation read in part: "Although severely wounded, [Lieutenant Sears] fought his battery until the cannoneers and horses were nearly all killed or wounded."

He recovered from his wounds and was promoted to lieutenant colonel "for gallant and meritorious conduct." Colonel Sears was placed in charge of the Eleventh Regiment, Louisiana Volunteers, later known as the Forty-ninth Regiment, United States Colored Infantry. He served with his new unit until being mustered out on March 22, 1866.

Shortly after the war, Cyrus married Sarah A. Harpster on May 27, 1865. Following his discharge, he returned to Upper Sandusky, where he resumed his legal profession. In 1876, Sears engaged himself in the mercantile trade in the new community of Fowler City. He would eventually operate a hotel and serve as postmaster for the town. He died on November 30, 1909, in Harpster. Several of his military mementos were donated to the Wyandot County Museum and can still be viewed today.

David Ayres Jr. (spelled Ayers on his official Medal of Honor record) was born on April 4, 1841, in Kalida, Ohio. By 1860, his family had moved to Upper

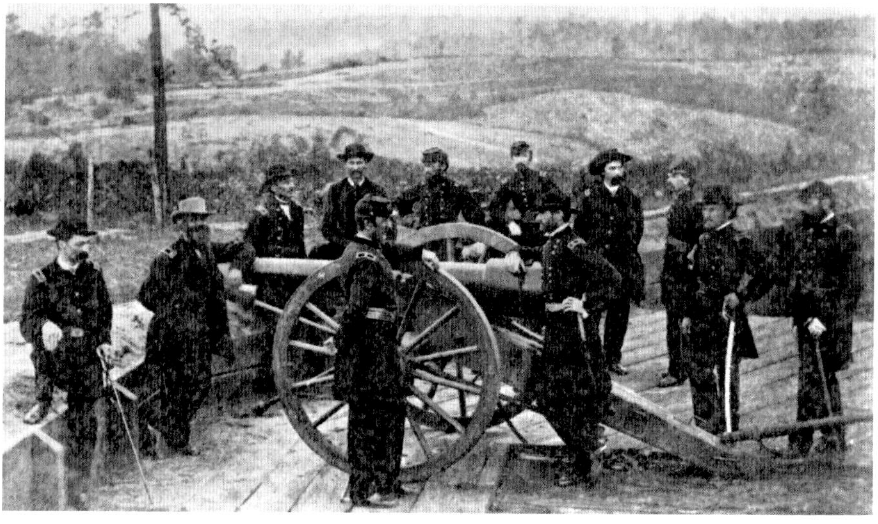

Civil War soldiers stand around a light artillery field piece similar to the ones commanded by Cyrus Sears at the Battle of Iuka, Mississippi. *Wyandot County Historical Society.*

Sandusky, where he enlisted in Company A, Fifty-seventh Regiment, Ohio Volunteer Infantry, on September 2, 1861. He was mustered in as a private on September 23 and was soon promoted to sergeant. Ayres was commissioned as a second lieutenant on February 3, 1863, prior to the Vicksburg Campaign but was not yet formally promoted at the time of the Battle of Vicksburg, Mississippi, on May 22, 1863. Next he was promoted to first lieutenant on August 16, 1864, and honorably discharged from the regiment on January 4, 1865. Ayres was recommissioned on April 15, 1865, into the Fifty-seventh Regiment's Company D. On August 10, 1865, he was promoted to captain but was mustered out of service five days later before his formal promotion ceremony.

Captain Ayres was awarded the Medal of Honor on August 13, 1894, for his actions as a sergeant during the Siege of Vicksburg in 1863. The official government citation reads simply that he was awarded for "gallantry in the charge of the 'volunteer storming party.'" Following the war, he moved to Pittsburg, Pennsylvania, where he worked in the mercantile trade and married Annie Elizabeth Crawford in 1870. The couple eventually had three children and later moved to Illinois. David died on December 11, 1916, in Chicago, Illinois, and was buried in Oak Woods Cemetery.

The Grand Army of the Republic was organized in Decatur, Illinois, by Benjamin F. Stevenson on April 6, 1866, to give the numerous Union veterans of the Civil War a place to meet, share stories and, more importantly, remember their fallen comrades. Several posts were formed in Wyandot County, and most erected an everlasting memorial in their community to honor the veterans even after the last survivor had passed on. By 1925, most of the local posts had closed due to the deaths of their members.

R. Robbins Post No. 91 was organized in Upper Sandusky on June 20, 1880, with thirteen original members and was chartered on January 17, 1881. It was named in honor of Major Rodolphus Robbins (Fifty-fifth Regiment, Ohio Volunteer Infantry), who was killed in action at Resaca, Georgia, on May 15, 1864.

The post had three primary memorials located throughout the city. The aforementioned Robbins' Rock in Harrison Smith Park was originally dedicated by the post in 1926 as a memorial to fellow members and to commemorate a section of parkland (including a picnic grove and shelter house) donated by the surviving members. The boulder was inscribed, "ROBBINS POST 91 GAR GROVE." During 2011, Eagle Scout Nick Reid cleaned the stone, as well as other memorials in the park. The Wyandot Memorial Association fenced in the boulder, added a bronze plaque and rededicated the memorial on October 29, 2011.

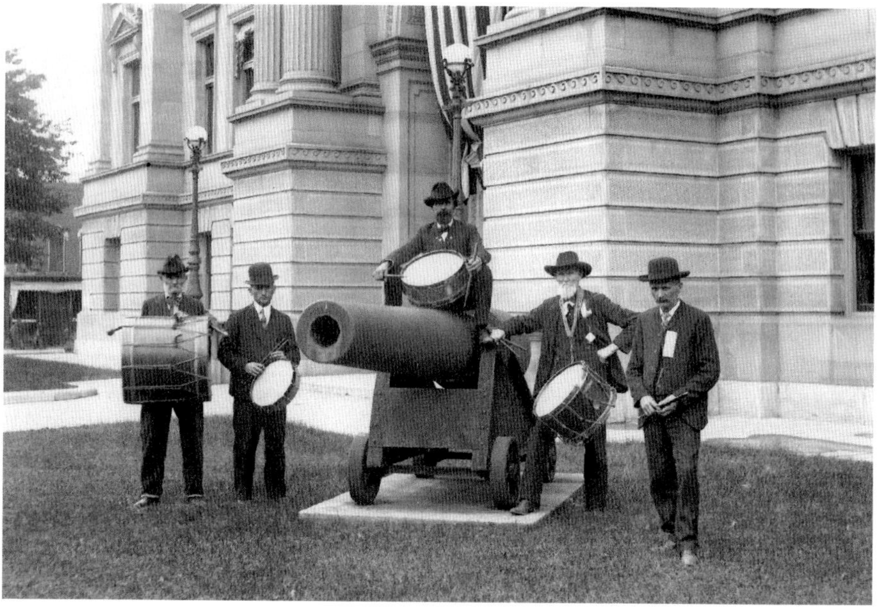

The Green River Band stands alongside one of the two Civil War cannons (Parrott rifles) in front of the Wyandot County Courthouse. *Wyandot County Historical Society.*

The 1861–65 Memorial Roll is a bronze plaque located on the rear wall underneath the main staircase in the Wyandot County Courthouse. It contains 281 names and is inscribed "TO CARE FOR HIM WHO HAS BORNE THE HEAT OF BATTLE AND FOR HIS WIDOW AND ORPHANS." It is possible this memorial was located in a more prominent position within the previous courthouse.

In 1900, the post arranged for two Parrott rifles from Fort Adams in Newport, Rhode Island, to be placed at the new courthouse. These obsolete siege cannons, weighing around nine thousand pounds each, were used along the coastline and were placed on loan from the U.S. Army to the local GAR post. They were delivered in July 1900 and placed on either side of the front entrance of the Wyandot County Courthouse. Limbaugh and O'Connor of Tiffin, Ohio, made the carriages for them to rest on. The cannons were dedicated during the courthouse ceremony on August 24, 1900.

In 1942, President Franklin Roosevelt called for all military field equipment memorials to be donated for the war effort. Since all members of the post were deceased, the local Spanish-American War Veterans' Camp donated the cannons in October 1942. They were taken to the Empire Steel Mill in Mansfield, Ohio. Supposedly, the mill was unable to melt them down and

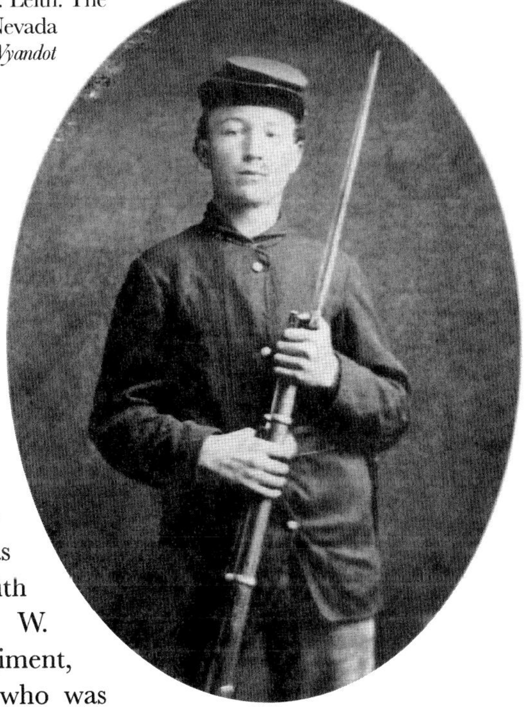
A carte de vista of Private Francis M. Leith. The Grand Army of the Republic post in Nevada was named for him and his brothers. *Wyandot County Historical Society.*

moved the old cannons to a scrapyard in the town. The final fate of the two cannons is unclear.

Leith Post No. 127 was organized by Colonel H.A. Brown in Nevada. It was chartered on August 24, 1881, with twenty-one members. The post was named in honor of the Leith brothers: Sergeant Owen W. Leith (Company E, 11th Regiment, Illinois Volunteer Infantry), who was killed during the Battle of Fort Donnellson, Tennessee, in February 1862; Private Francis M. Leith (Company K, 55th Regiment, Ohio Volunteer Infantry), who was killed in Magnolia, North Carolina, on April 2, 1865; and Private Isaac Lowery Leith (Company I, 15th Regiment, Ohio Volunteer Infantry), who was killed near Dallas, Georgia, on May 28, 1864. Their cousin First Lieutenant James Steele Leith (Company H, 144th Regiment, Ohio Volunteer Infantry) survived the war and became a charter member of the post.

In 1904, the post erected a seven-foot-tall, three-foot-wide sandstone monument with a decorative ball on top in Nevada Cemetery. The ball has since been removed, and it now rests on the ground to the left of the memorial. Several Civil War veterans' grave markers are located near it.

Colonel Crawford Post No. 173 was organized in Carey on December 16, 1881, with sixteen charter members. It was named in honor of Colonel William Crawford, who was executed by the Delaware Nation on June 11, 1782. There are two memorials associated with the camp.

The Carey Cannon is a three inch ordnance rifle manufactured by the Phoenix Iron Company of Phoenixville, Pennsylvania, in 1862. The cannon was also known as a ten-pounder due to the size of the shells it fired. The artillery piece sat dormant in the village park for several years until a group of Civil War enthusiasts restored the cannon and constructed a carriage for it. Now the old memorial is used at reenactments and for public demonstrations by Battery H, First Ohio Volunteer Artillery. The Carey Ladies' Auxiliary Corps erected a four-foot square granite marker in Spring Grove Cemetery during 1912. The memorial dedicated to the Carey Post was erected on a plot owned by the post. It includes an engraving of a GAR badge and was inscribed, "IN MEMORY OF THE DEPARTED COMRADES OF 1861–1865."

Jaqueth Post No. 196 was originally organized in Sycamore by Inspector Brown of Toledo on January 31, 1882, with thirteen charter members. On July 10, 1883, due to some internal disagreements, the post disbanded. It was reorganized on June 26, 1885, with twenty members. The post was named in honor of Private Henry P. Jaqueth (Company K, Forty-ninth Regiment, Ohio Volunteer Infantry), who was killed on May 27, 1864, in the Battle at Pickett's Mills, Georgia. He originally enlisted in Captain Kirby's "Warpole Guards" in 1861. After serving his three months (April 20, 1861, to August 28, 1861) in the Fifteenth Regiment, he enlisted as a private in the Forty-ninth Regiment on February 27, 1862. Henry was promoted to corporal on March 1, 1864.

The members erected an eight-foot-tall, four-foot-wide rectangular granite monument in Old Sycamore Cemetery. The irregularly carved stone included an image of an American flag and was inscribed, "IN MEMORY OF THE HEROES WHO GAVE THEIR LIVES THAT THE UNION MIGHT LIVE." Several Civil War veterans' grave markers surround the memorial.

Wilkerson Post No. 264 was organized in Wharton on September 28, 1882, with twenty-two charter members. The post was named in honor of musician Thomas Wilkerson Petty (Company I, Forty-ninth Regiment, Ohio Volunteer Infantry), who was killed at the Battle of Nashville, Tennessee, on December 16, 1864. He enlisted as a private on August 3, 1861, and was promoted to principal musician on September 1, 1864.

Ellis Post No. 292 was chartered in Marseilles on February 2, 1883. The post was named in honor of Corporal Benjamin Ellis, who enlisted with Company D, Eighty-first Regiment, Ohio Volunteer Infantry, on September 28, 1861. Wounded during battle, he was discharged on January 15, 1863, with a surgeon's Certificate of Disability. Ellis returned to Marseilles and took up the occupation of carpenter until his death on March 18, 1881. Interestingly, his father, John Ellis, served under General Anthony Wayne from 1793 to 1795 and participated in the Battle of Fallen Timbers.

The primary memorial for the camp is the Marseilles Cannon located in Chandler Cemetery near Marseilles. It is officially known as a three-inch ordnance rifle, sometimes called a ten-pounder. It was manufactured by the Phoenix Iron Company about 1862. After many years in the elements, its carriage finally deteriorated, and the cannon was placed in storage for safekeeping. During the 1990s, students in Ray Gottfried's Industrial Arts Class at Upper Sandusky High School created a new carriage and placed the cannon back to its place of honor in the cemetery.

A group of local veterans and military-minded men from Upper Sandusky formed the Kirby Light Guards in 1877. These men participated in parades, military remembrances and local patriotic celebrations. Later, the Kirby Light Guards became loosely affiliated with the state militia. On February 15, 1898, the USS *Maine* was blown up in Havana Harbor. This action was blamed on Spain and led to the United States signing a declaration of war against Spain on April 22, 1898.

When President William McKinley called for men to volunteer for the Spanish-American War in 1898, this group of guards was among the first

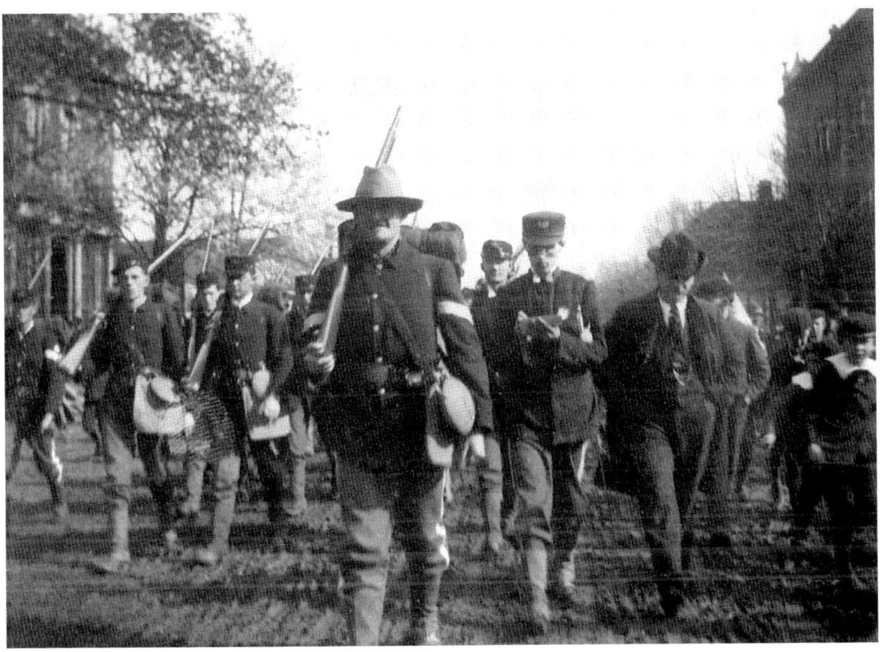

Sergeant Avery Peters leads soldiers of Company B, Second Regiment, Ohio National Guard, who served in the Spanish-American War, as they march through the county. *Wyandot County Historical Society.*

to be called. The men, primarily from Upper Sandusky and Carey, were enlisted into the Ohio National Guard. Wyandot County sent 103 men to form the basis of Company B, Second Regiment, Ohio National Guard. On April 25, 1898, the regiment, part of the Third Brigade, Second Division, First Army Corps, was mustered into active service at Kenton.

The men departed for Columbus, Ohio, two days later and were eventually stationed at the former Civil War battlefield near Chickamauga, Georgia. Similar to men in many other National Guard units, they were never stationed overseas. Following numerous illnesses at the Georgia site, in August 1898, the regiment was relocated to Knoxville, Tennessee, where it stayed until the peace treaty was ratified by the Senate in February 1899. Company B was mustered out at Macon, Georgia, on February 10, 1899, and returned home two days later having lost only two men. According to an article in the *University Herald* (Ada, Ohio) on November 17, 1899, the Second Regiment, Ohio National Guard, was reorganized into the following companies composed of men from the associated towns: A-Findlay, B-Carey, C-Lima, E-Tiffin, F-Belle Center, G-Ada, H-Bloomdale, I-Kenton and L-Wapakoneta. Many of these units were active until the army was reorganized during World War I.

In 1904, the United Spanish War Veterans organization was organized by men who had served in the Spanish-American War, Philippine Insurrection and China Relief Expedition fought between 1898 and 1902. The Byron Baguley Camp No. 73 United Spanish War Veterans was organized in Upper Sandusky. It was named in honor of Henry Byron Baguley, a medical doctor who was the chief surgeon of the First Regiment, West Virginia Volunteer Infantry. He was stationed with the Second Brigade at Chickamauga and treated many of the sick men from Wyandot County. He died in Wheeling, West Virginia, on May 1, 1908, and was fondly remembered by the men for whom he had cared. In 1928, the members of Camp No. 73 erected a brick monument in Harrison Smith Park dedicated to Company B. It contains a porthole cover from the USS *Maine*.

Unlike for previous conflicts, during World War I, there were no units raised completely of men from Wyandot County. A draft system was instituted to fill the ranks of the reorganized U.S. military. Following the declaration of war against Germany on April 6, 1917, thousands of men swelled the ranks of the military with over 16.3 million service personnel seeing action.

Over 6,500 Ohio men lost their lives during the Great War with the county recording the loss of only 23 men. Private George Bolyard was the

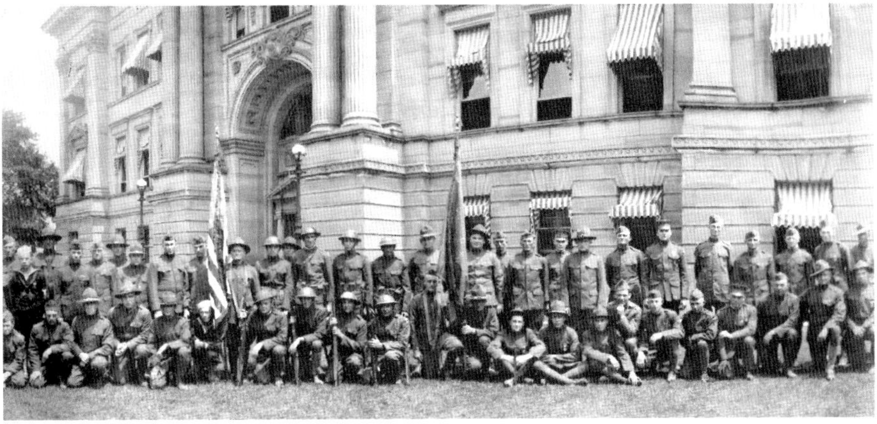

Following World War I, county veterans from all branches gathered in front of the Wyandot County Courthouse for a group photograph. *Wyandot County Historical Society*.

first Wyandot County resident killed in the line of duty during the war, and Private Mendus Hart was the last recorded combat death. On November 11, 1918, an armistice was signed formally ending the war.

In September 1939, Germany invaded Poland, beginning a second major war that would involve most of Europe. Despite two of America's major allies, France and England, being attacked, the United States remained uninvolved for the most part in World War II. Most Americans also took little notice of Japanese activities in the Pacific. This all changed on December 7, 1941, when Japan attacked Pearl Harbor on the island of Oahu, Hawaii. Within days, the United States had declared war against Japan, Germany and their allied countries.

A draft lottery was instituted with names and numbers of county men printed in the Upper Sandusky *Daily Chief-Union*, among other local newspapers. Numerous county men and women enlisted for service, allowing them to choose how they wished to serve rather than waiting to be called up. Most joined the army and navy while the residents left behind filled their factory and labor jobs. A small group of local women enlisted in the WACs (Women's Army Corps), WASPs (Women Airforce Service Pilots) and WAVES (Women Accepted for Volunteer Emergency Service), as well as in the nursing corps. Military personnel from the county saw service in every major theater of action, including the Battle of the Bulge, Iwo Jima and D-Day.

Like in every other county in America, rationing took effect here during the course of World War II. Items like sugar, coffee, meat, tires and gasoline were in limited supply. Scrap drives were common. Industrious residents grew their own vegetable gardens and reused as many items as possible. Despite these limitations, the county survived the war with few major impacts. The conflict lasted nearly four years, and on May 7, 1945, Germany surrendered. V-E (Victory in Europe) Day was declared on May 25, 1945. Two atomic bombs were dropped on Japan in August 1945, leading to V-J

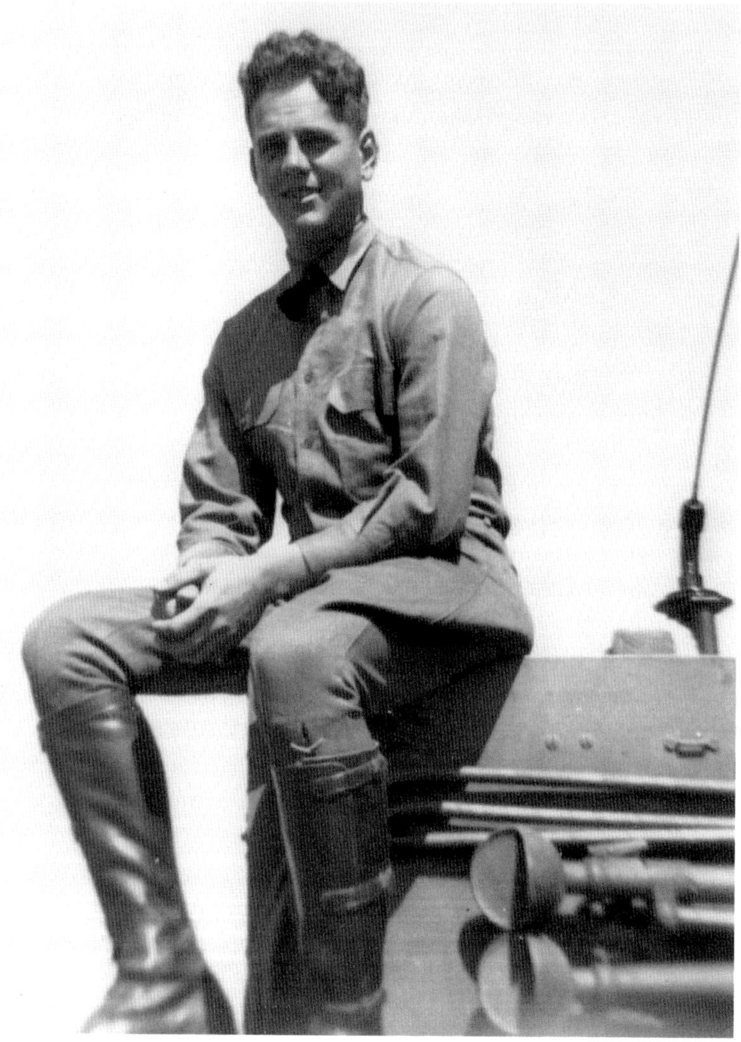

An image of Private William Kraus, who served in the Army National Guard during World War II with Company C, Twenty-second Cavalry Division. *Wyandot County Historical Society.*

(Victory over Japan) Day being declared on August 16, 1945. Following this action, a two-day holiday was declared in Wyandot County to celebrate the end of the war. The war was finally considered complete when Japan signed an unconditional surrender aboard the USS *Missouri* on September 2, 1945. Cessation of hostilities was not formally declared until December 31, 1946.

Approximately 641,000 Ohioans served during the war. Of these, 2,169 men and women were from Wyandot County. Private Foster Steif was the first Wyandot County resident to lose his life during the war, and Second Lieutenant John Byers was the last recorded death. On October 13, 2013, the Wyandot Memorial Association erected in Upper Sandusky's Bicentennial Park a granite monument dedicated to the men and women who served, as well as the 60 county residents who gave their lives.

Only five years after the end of World War II, the United States again found itself in conflict on foreign soil. Following the invasion of South Korea by North Korea, the United States supported its ally by declaring war on North Korea on June 25, 1950. The back-and-forth conflict between the forces of the United States and South Korea against North Korea and China raged until a cease-fire was declared on July 27, 1953. This agreement created along the thirty-eighth parallel a new border known as the Demilitarized Zone. In 2013, the sixtieth anniversary of the world's longest-lasting cease-fire agreement was observed.

Of the 1,771 Ohioans to die during the Korean War, only three (Ensign John Frederick Kail, Private First Class James Elwood Gatchel and Master Sergeant Harold M. Swihart) from the county were killed in action. On July 31, 2010, the Wyandot County Vietnam Traveling Wall Foundation erected a polished black granite monument in Bicentennial Park in memory of the county veterans who served during the Korean War.

Thomas J. Swinehart is the only local Korean War veteran known to be awarded the Prisoner of War Medal following his capture in North Korea in 1952. He was born on December 24, 1931, in Wyandot County. On February 29, 1952, Swinehart enlisted in the U.S. Army. He was assigned to the Fortieth Infantry Division. During maneuvers, he was captured by the enemy on October 31, 1952. He was held in captivity until September 3, 1953. According to military records, upon his return to American troops, the military considered his enlistment fulfilled, and he was soon honorably discharged. Eventually, he returned to Upper Sandusky, where he died on October 27, 2009, and was buried in the Nevada Cemetery.

Quite possibly the greatest event to shape the latter half of the twentieth century was the Vietnam War. Its effect was felt around the world and into the small towns, schools and hearts of all Wyandot Countians. Protests for and against the war were held around the nation with strong opinions on both sides. Another generation of young men and women was pressed into military service through enlistment and the draft. The last official draft lottery was conducted on December 31, 1969. Whether they entered the military through voluntary enlistment or the draft, the men and women of Wyandot County honorably served their country during the course of the war.

The Vietnam War began in 1955 following tensions between France and North Vietnam during the First Indochina War; however, American involvement was primarily as military advisor until 1964. Congress signed the Gulf of Tonkin Resolution on August 7, 1964, authorizing combat operations in Vietnam, although air strikes had already started two days earlier. The first official American combat boots did not hit the ground until March 8, 1965, at China Beach near Da Nang, South Vietnam. On April 30, 1975, the last American soldiers and advisors left the U.S. embassy in Saigon. A week later, on May 7, President Gerald Ford declared the official end of the war. Over 9 million American military service personnel served during the war with 3,094 deaths of Ohioans. Over 800 local residents participated with 11 men sacrificing their lives in the line of duty. This list includes Communications Technician Second Class Stephen Joseph Tesmer, who was the last recorded resident from the county to die in armed conflict in April 1969.

Accompanied by a motorcycle escort, the American Veterans Traveling Tribute arrived in Upper Sandusky on May 11, 2005. A group later known as the Wyandot County Vietnam Traveling Wall Foundation arranged for the display of the four-fifths-scale replica of the Vietnam Veterans Memorial. This activity inspired the Wyandot County Vietnam Memorial in Bicentennial Park, which was dedicated on May 13, 2006. The polished black granite monument lists the names of 335 county veterans on the left panel, 494 names on the right panel and the names of the 11 men who sacrificed their lives on the center panel.

On August 2, 1990, Iraq forces under the command of President Saddam Hussein invaded its tiny neighbor Kuwait. This action was swiftly condemned by the United Nations General Assembly. American troops arrived in Saudi Arabia shortly afterward, leading to the formation of the defensive-minded Operation Desert Shield on August 7, 1990. Additional troops from the United States and allied countries arrived over the course of the next few months, creating a coalition of thirty-nine nations. Several thousand Ohioans served with only sixteen reported deaths. As in all

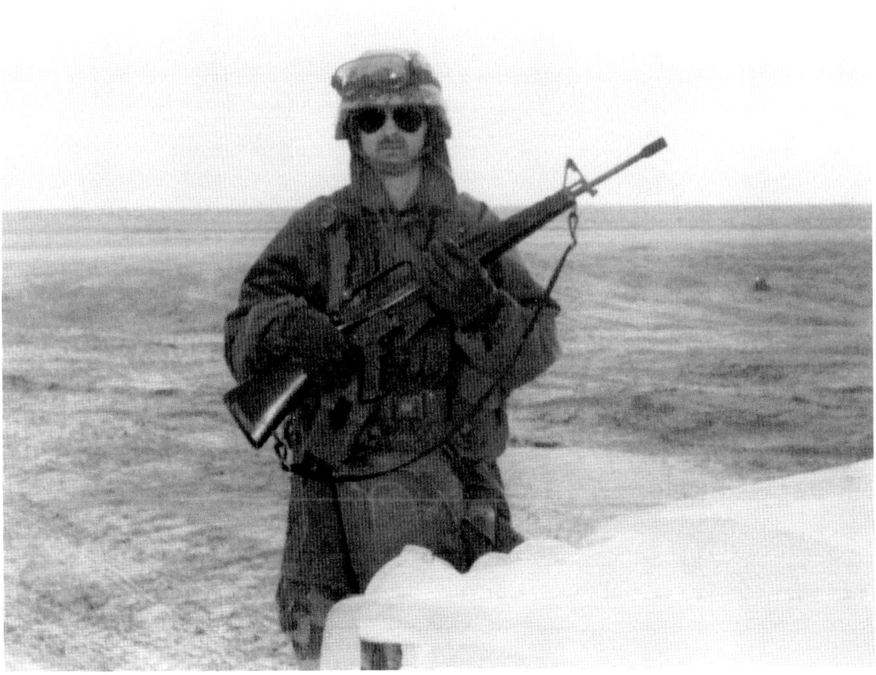

Specialist Ronald Marvin Jr. served as a terrain analyst with the First Infantry Division during Operation Desert Shield and Operation Desert Storm. *Author's collection.*

previous wars, Wyandot County residents participated, although in much smaller numbers than ever before due to an all-volunteer military.

On November 29, 1990, the United Nations Security Council Resolution 678 authorized military action to evict Iraq. Operation Desert Storm officially began on January 17, 1991, with an air campaign. On February 24, a one-hundred-hour ground war occurred that expelled the Iraqi troops and liberated Kuwait. A cease-fire was signed on February 28, 1991. The United Nations declared an official end to the war on April 11, 1991, and the American troops began to return home.

One of the most tragic events of the new century occurred on September 11, 2001, when the World Trade Center Towers in New York City were destroyed by commercial airliners in the deadliest terrorist attack on American soil. An airplane also hit the Pentagon, and another crashed near Shanksville, Pennsylvania. These attacks stirred up patriotism in the young people of the county, leading several to enter military service as part of the new War on Terror that replaced the long-running cold war.

Three days after the 9/11 attack, Congress authorized the use of military force against the perpetrators, led by Osama Bin Laden, who were reportedly hiding in Afghanistan. This action led to America's longest-lasting war. On October 7, 2001, Operation Enduring Freedom, commonly known as the Afghanistan War, began. The campaign continued until December 28, 2014, when it was succeeded by Operation Freedom's Sentinel on January 1, 2015. Approximately 1,742 men and women died during the war, including nearly 100 Ohioans, none of whom were from the county.

The Iraq War, which deposed Saddam Hussein, was authorized by Congress on October 16, 2002. It began on March 19, 2003, and combat operations were concluded on May 1. Operation Iraqi Freedom, as it was officially known, continued until August 31, 2010, when it was replaced by Operation New Dawn. Even though some Americans troops would remain as advisors, the war officially ended on December 15, 2011. Nearly two hundred Ohioans died during combat operations in Iraq. Thankfully, Wyandot County did not lose anyone during battle. Continuing the tradition of military service from the earliest days of the county, several hundred men and women are currently serving in America's armed forces.

9

That Championship Feeling

During the last one hundred years, many local students have found great success playing high school sports. Most teams played intramural games in the early years and then progressed to interscholastic games. These gave a sense of pride to the schools and led to great rivalries over the ensuing years. Most of the early high schools joined the Wyandot County League and played for local trophies and bragging rights. It was not until November 1907 that the Ohio High School Athletic Association (OHSAA) was established. Eventually, state playoffs would be established in several team sports in which the local schools participated. The following is a brief look at some of the state championship and "final four" teams. In addition, a number of individual athletes found success in their respective sports. In the last half of the 1900s, most of the small high schools consolidated until only three were left in the county.

During the early 1900s, baseball was the primary sport played in the country. Football and basketball were in their infancy, and their professional leagues would not catch on until the middle and latter half of the century Many local boys played the game, and a few attained great skill, ultimately playing at the highest level. At least two locals made it into the ranks of Major League Baseball during its early years.

William Edgar Hahn was born on August 27, 1875, in Nevada, Ohio. Like most children in the area, he learned to play baseball at a young age. By 1900, he was playing on championship teams in the Nevada area. He began playing professional baseball about 1902 with the New Orleans Pelicans of the Cotton

States League. Hahn attracted the attention of the New York Highlanders of the American League, who purchased his contract in August 1905. He made his major-league debut on August 31. After a poor start in 1906, the right fielder was sold to the Chicago White Sox, who won the pennant that year.

The White Sox faced the favored Chicago Cubs in the World Series. William was the team's leadoff hitter and, as such, was the first batter to appear at the plate during the series. He went hitless in the first two games and then, when he was hit in the face in the next game, broke his nose. Undaunted, Hahn returned to the lineup in game four, going six for fourteen the rest of the series. He scored two runs in both games five and six, leading the White Sox to their first World Series crown.

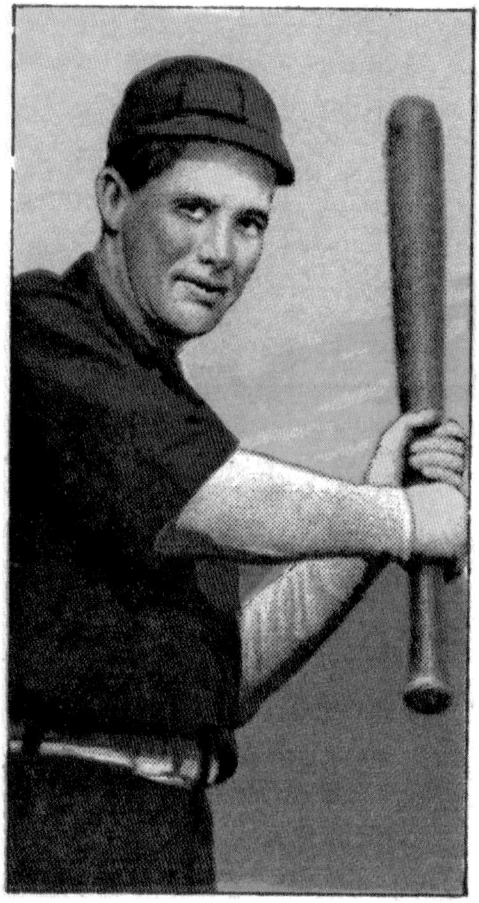

The American Tobacco Company produced this 1909 baseball card of Ed Hahn, who played professionally with the Chicago White Sox from 1906 to 1910. *Wyandot County Historical Society.*

Hahn had his best year statistically in 1907, finishing in the top five in several categories, including runs scored, walks and hit by pitch while leading all outfielders with a .990 fielding percentage. Over the next few years, he did not achieve the same success, and by 1910, he had been sent down to the minors. The year 1911 found him in the Ohio-Pennsylvania League as a player-manager with the Mansfield Brownies. His last five years in organized baseball were with the Des Moines Boosters of the Western League. Upon his retirement, he took a job as a night watchman at a cement company. Hahn died on November 29, 1941, in Des Moines, Iowa.

Wilfred Pearl Osborn was born on November 28, 1883, in Nevada, Ohio. Nicknamed "Ossie," he learned baseball at an early age and, by 1900, was playing on championship teams in Nevada. His ability as a player caught the attention of minor-league teams. He began his professional career as an outfielder with Canton of the Central League. The Chicago Cubs purchased the centerfielder for $2,000 in August 1905. He stayed with the team for two years until being sold in June 1907 to the Philadelphia Phillies. Osborn made his major-league debut on June 8, 1907, and played with the franchise for three years. His best year statistically was 1908, as he played in his most games and finished first among all major-league outfielders in outfield putouts. He played his last game on July 24, 1909. Following his baseball career, he returned to Wyandot County and died on September 2, 1954, in Upper Sandusky.

Boys, and occasionally girls, loved to emulate their major-league heroes with amateur pickup games nearly every day during the warmer months. These teams soon found their way into the local school playgrounds and surrounding fields. As a result, almost every high school sponsored a baseball team, and these often faced one another for regional titles. The Ohio High

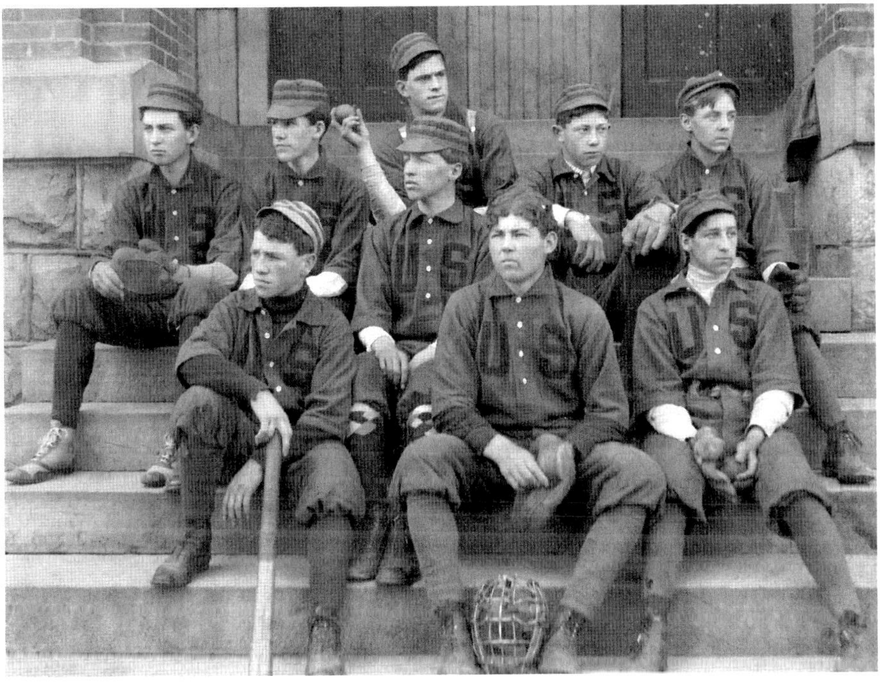

Local photographer Harry Kinley captured this image of the 1901 Upper Sandusky High School baseball team, in uniform with gear. *Wyandot County Historical Society*.

School Athletic Association began hosting playoffs for the burgeoning sport of baseball in 1928, dividing the teams into two divisions.

McCutchenville High School was the first local team to advance to the state championship round in 1948. McCutchenville participated in the small school Class B tournament. The team lost in the state semifinals 8–6 to state runner-up Galena Orange High School. The following year, the school became the first in the county to appear in a state championship game. Coach Merl Rosendale led the team to the 1949 Class B title game. The Big Red defeated Wickliff High School 4–1 in the semifinals. Unfortunately, McCutchenville lost 3–2 in the state championship game on May 28, 1949, to Taylor-Cleves High School.

For the third consecutive year, McCutchenville High School advanced to the Class B state final four in baseball. The team lost 6–2 in the 1950 semifinals to state runner-up Middleport High School. Two years later, in 1952, the Big Red once more advanced to the state championship round. Unfortunately, the squad lost again in the semifinals. This time, the score was 6–3 in favor of eventual state champion Beavercreek High School. McCutchenville never reached the title round again and, in 1962, was consolidated with Upper Sandusky High School.

In 1954, Sycamore High School, coached by Henry Roberson, made a deep run in the state tournament. After finishing undefeated in the regular season, the Wildcats made the playoffs by defeating every team placed in their path. In the state semifinals, they defeated Salem Local High School 4–0 to meet Waverly High School in the state championship game. After leading 1–0 going into the bottom of the final inning, the team gave up two runs, which cost them the title. Sycamore finished 20-1 for the season and was the Class B runner-up.

The following year, the team returned to the baseball final four. The Wildcats faced Class B state runner-up Dublin High School in the semifinals and were defeated 5–4. Sycamore High School was the last county team to advance to the baseball championships, although Sycamore Mohawk High School would later have great success in the softball tournament.

Boys' track and field was actually the first state championship to be sanctioned by the new Ohio High School Athletic Association. Originally, due to the small number of member schools, all the high schools would compete against one another regardless of size. In 1921, the schools were separated into two divisions: Class A for large schools and Class B for small schools. The girls' track and field tournament was not established, with three divisions, until 1975. In 1990, the names of the divisions were changed from A, AA, AAA to I, II, III.

The first school in the county to actually win an OHSAA state championship was the Nevada High School Boys' Track and Field team in 1954. The squad did not have an official track at its high school, but Coach Alvin Buckeye did not let that deter the team. According to local stories, the boys ran around the school and practiced on its playground. They substituted barrels for hurdles, used cement blocks to practice throwing the shot put and drilled holes in the ground to practice the pole vault. Their unique efforts were successful, as they won the Class B title 18–16 over Cuyahoga Heights High School with Jim Steinhilber and Jim Stiger capturing individual titles.

It was not until 2000 that the next state championship track team appeared in the county. Head coach Jim Clifford led the Upper Sandusky High School Girls' Track and Field team to the 2000 Division II state title. The Rams defeated runner-up Dayton Dunbar High School 59–26 at the state track championships held in June at Dayton's Welcome Stadium. They were led by the first-place finishes of Jessica Falk, Danielle Gottfried, Meghan Horn, Kehly Amesquita and Emily Herring.

The team successfully defended its title at the 2001 state championship track meet. New head coach Tim Pohlman directed the Upper Sandusky High School Girls' Track and Field team to the Division II state title. The squad defeated runner-up Columbus School for Girls 31–28 at the state track championships again held in June at Welcome Stadium. It was led by Meghan Horn's second of three straight state titles in the shot put.

After nearly seventy years of declaring state champions in football by acclimation or poll, the OHSAA instituted a playoff system with three separate divisions to determine a champion on the field. In 1975, Carey High School played in the small school division. The team won its first seven games before suffering its lone loss. Coach Tom Geschwind led the team to an 8-1 regular season record and its first North Central Conference championship. The Blue Devils defeated Burton Berkshire High School 26–24 at Mansfield, Ohio, to make the championship game. Needing overtime, Carey defeated the previously unscored on Newark Catholic High School in the Akron Rubber Bowl to capture the Class A state title.

Nearly twenty years later, Carey High School once again advanced to the state championship round. Coach Jim Draper led the Blue Devils to an undefeated season and the Midland Athletic League championship in only their fifth year in the conference. The squad won its first playoff game, earning a spot in the Division V state semifinals at Lima Stadium. Carey lost 14–0 to the eventually undefeated state champion Versailles High School. Although Upper Sandusky and Sycamore Mohawk have appeared in the

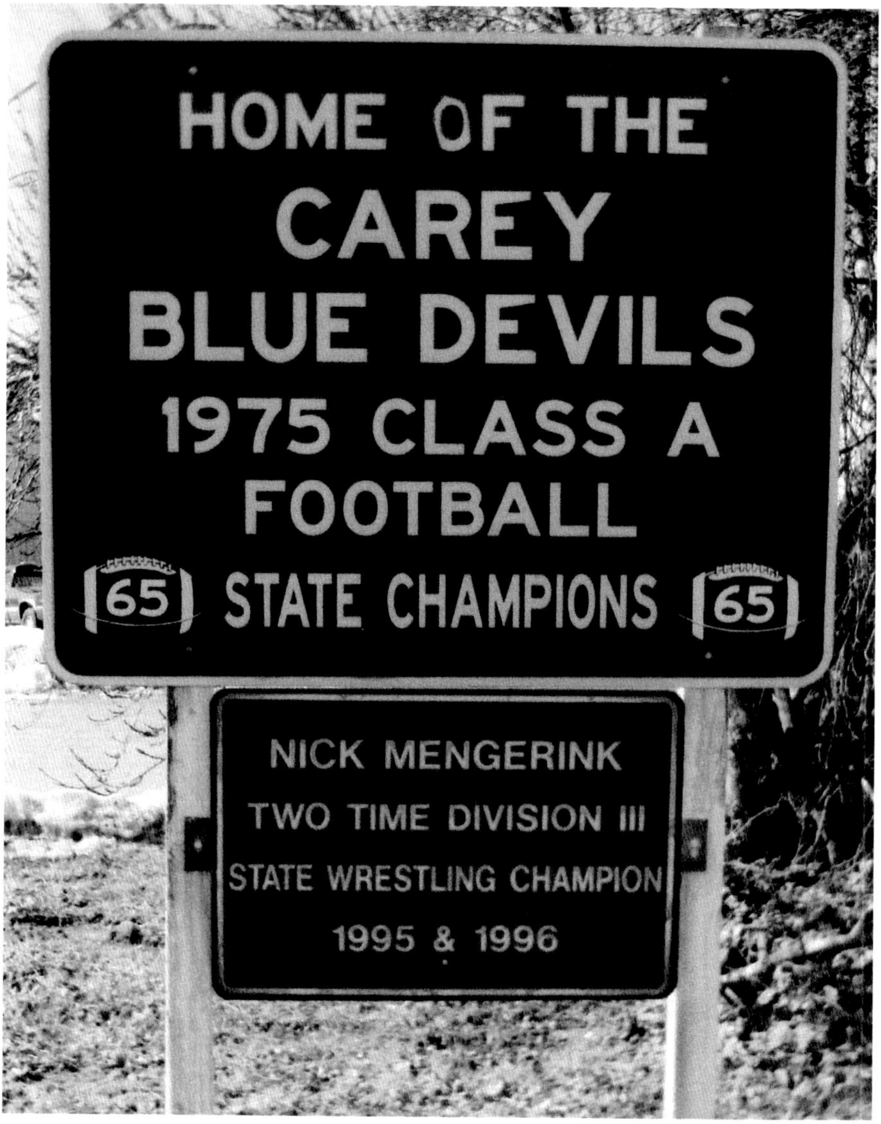

A sign along State Route 199 at the edge of Carey proclaiming the local high school's lone state championship football team and local wresting champion. *Author's collection.*

football playoffs, Carey remains the only county high school to play in the final four.

A little over thirty years after the boys of Sycamore High School found success in the state baseball tournament, the girls of Sycamore Mohawk

High School reached the state championship round. Despite softball having been played for several years, the state did not establish a tournament until 1978. For the first twenty-three years, there were three divisions. In 2001, a fourth division was created.

Sycamore Mohawk High School made its first appearance in the state championship round in 1988. Coach Carl Long led the team to the Class A semifinals, which it lost to state runner-up Portsmouth Clay High School. The Warriors, led again by Coach Long, returned to the final four in 1994. Mohawk defeated Pleasant Hill Newton High School 3–2 to advance to the Division III state title game. The team lost the

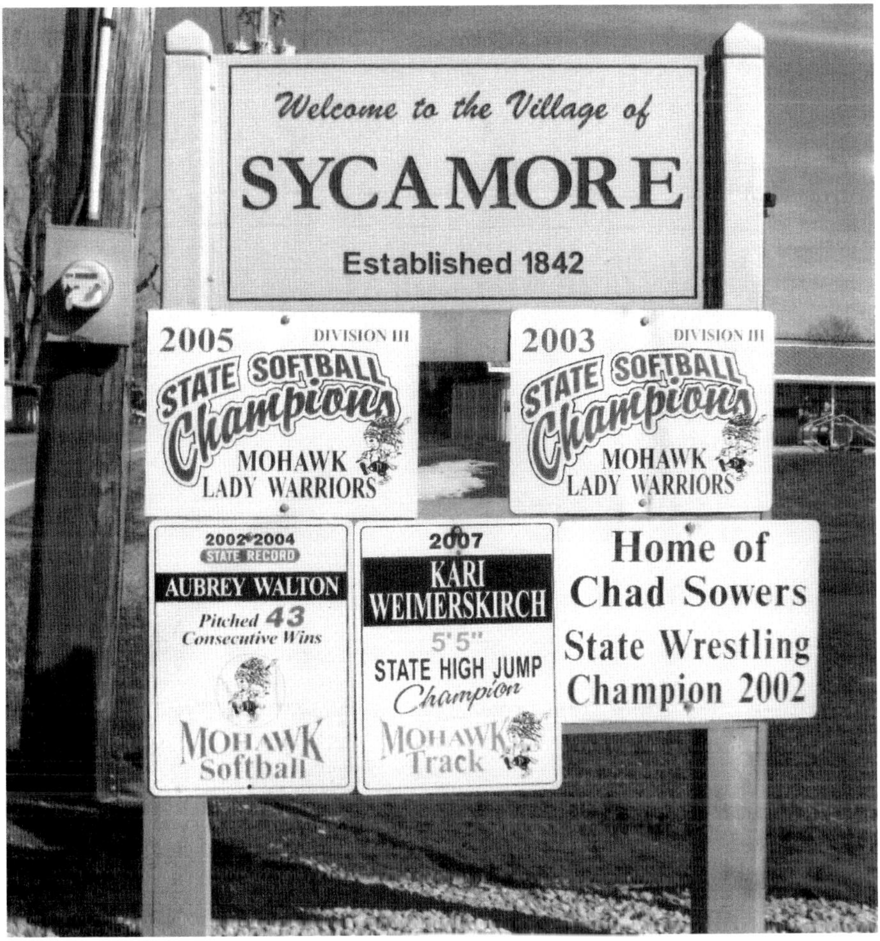

A sign along State Route 103 at the edge of Sycamore listing multiple individual and state championships won by Mohawk High School athletes. *Author's collection.*

championship 3–2 in eight innings to Jeromesville Hillsdale High School to finish with a 23-4 record.

In 2003, the school captured its first state championship ever. Head Coach Jenny Weinandy guided Sycamore Mohawk back to the state final four. The team was led by pitcher Aubrey Walton, who was in the midst of a school record 43-game winning streak during this season. The squad defeated Rootstown High School 5–0 in the semifinals. It captured the 2003 Division III state title with a 6–1 victory over Convoy Crestview High School at Brookside Park in Ashland, Ohio, on June 7, 2003, to finish 30-1 on the season.

Two years later, Sycamore Mohawk, under the continued leadership of Head Coach Jenny Weinandy, won its second state championship in softball. Following another successful regular season, the Warriors advanced through the playoffs until they reached the state championship round in Ashland. The squad defeated Leavittsburg LaBrae High School 8–6 in the semifinals. Mohawk scored one run in the bottom of the first inning to squeak by Chillicothe Zane Trace High School 1–0 and capture the Division III state title on June 4, 2005. The Warriors completed their season with a 31-2 record.

As basketball began to transform from an exercise class at local high schools to organized games, many schools established teams leading to the Wyandot County League. Eventually, the Ohio High School Athletic Association established playoffs for boys' basketball in 1927 and girls' basketball in 1976.

The first girls' basketball team to advance to the OHSAA state championship round was the 1982 Upper Sandusky High School squad. Head Coach Andra Bell led the Lady Rams to a 17-3 record in the regular season before embarking on a long postseason run. The team lost 49–36 to state runner-up Cincinnati Reading High School in the state semifinals at Columbus. In 1991, Upper Sandusky High School, under the leadership of Coach Andra Bell, returned to the Division III state championship round in Columbus. The team lost to eventual state champion Dayton Dunbar High School 79–43 to finish with a record of 20-6.

Five years later, Coach Andra Bell directed the Lady Rams to an undefeated regular season. The Upper Sandusky High School girls' basketball team advanced to the Division III state final four in 1996. The team defeated Sugarcreek Garaway High School 63–57 in the semifinals at Columbus to advance to the championship game. Upper Sandusky lost to Cincinnati Wyoming High School 35–29 in overtime to finish its season at 27-1.

In 2009, Carey High School became the second county school to appear in the girls' basketball championship round at Value City Arena in Columbus. Coach Phil Vaughn led his squad to Division IV state semifinals, where they faced state runner-up Berlin Hiland High School. The Blue Devils lost 73–42 on March 19, 2009, to finish with a 23-3 record.

The first boys' basketball team from Wyandot County to reach the state final four was Upper Sandusky High School in 2005. This was also the most successful basketball squad to ever play in the county. Head Coach Keith Diebler led the Rams to an undefeated regular season. They rolled through the playoffs, qualifying for the Division II state final four at Value City Arena in Columbus. In the semifinals the team defeated Dayton Dunbar High School 95–90 to advance to the championship game. On March 19, 2005, Jon Diebler's 32 points led the team as Upper Sandusky defeated Wooster Triway High School 94–86 to win its first state title and finish a 27-0 undefeated season.

Two years later, the Upper Sandusky High School boys' basketball team returned to the Division II state championship round in Columbus under the direction of Coach Keith Diebler. The squad defeated Poland Seminary High School 89–58 in the semifinals to advance to the state title game. Despite

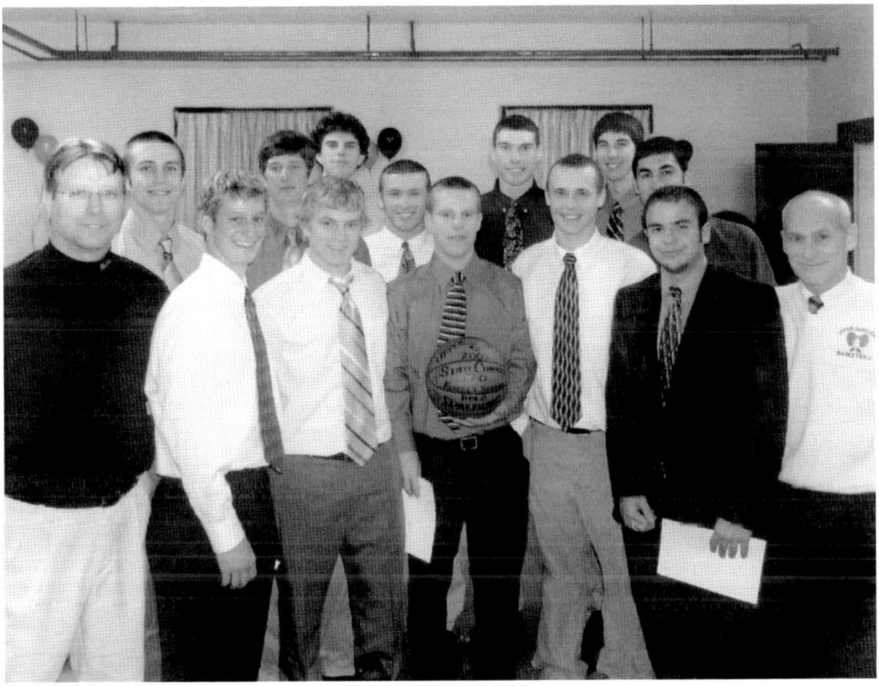

Members of the undefeated 2005 Upper Sandusky High School state championship basketball team. The autographed ball is on display at the Wyandot County Museum. *Wyandot County Historical Society.*

Jon Diebler's 48 points, Upper Sandusky lost the championship game 87–85 to Dayton Dunbar High School on March 4, 2007. The Rams finished their season with a 23-4 record. A standout at The Ohio State University, Diebler would go on to play professional basketball in Europe.

Volleyball is a sport that has been played for many years by young women in the county but has only recently achieved success at the state level. The state tournament is relatively young, having been established in 1975 with three divisions. In 1990, the state added a division and changed the classifications from A, AA, AAA to I, II, III, IV.

Sycamore Mohawk High School became the first county school to advance to the state volleyball final four in 2011. The team under the direction of Head Coach Eric Hoover finished second in the Midland Conference. It faced eventual state champion St. Henry High School in the Division IV semifinals. The Warriors lost a heartbreaking match in five sets on November 11 at the Ervin J. Nutter Center in Dayton to finish the season with a record of 25-3.

Two years later, Upper Sandusky High School made its first appearance in the state volleyball championship round. The Lady Rams, led by head coach Matthew McConnaughy, won the North Central Conference title. Advancing through the state tournament, they faced eventual champion Versailles High School in the 2013 Division III state semifinals. They fell in four sets on November 8 at the Nutter Center to finish their season at 25-3.

10

Remembering the Past

Curtis Berry, a local lawyer, originated the idea of marking the site of Colonel William Crawford's execution with a stone monument. During his remarks, Berry credited John Gormley with suggesting the monument's design, which called for a sandstone marker about eight and a half feet tall worked into the shape of an upright cannon. Sandstone from Berea, Ohio, was selected, and workers at B.L. Bauscher's firm in Upper Sandusky performed the stone cutting during the summer of 1877. The monument was placed on a bluff to the south of Tymochtee Creek on lands owned by Alfred K. Davis. The dedication ceremony was held on August 30, 1877, and nearly eight thousand persons attended before retiring for a "basket dinner." For many years afterward, the Pioneer Association of Wyandot County held its annual Pioneer Picnic at the monument or a small park near Crawford. The loss of the early pioneers and lack of interest in the next generation eventually led to the end of the picnics in 1935.

Visitors continued to flock to the monument, and it became a well-known tourist destination in the county despite being located on private property. Numerous problems with visitors in the 1970s and 1980s led to its access being restricted. The original monument was listed on the National Register of Historic Places on April 15, 1982.

In 1993, a group of concerned citizens met to discuss the possibility of erecting a new, publicly accessible monument to Crawford. The Wyandot County Patriotic Citizens group was formed and raised funds for a new eight-and-a-half-foot-tall monument virtually identical to the original to be

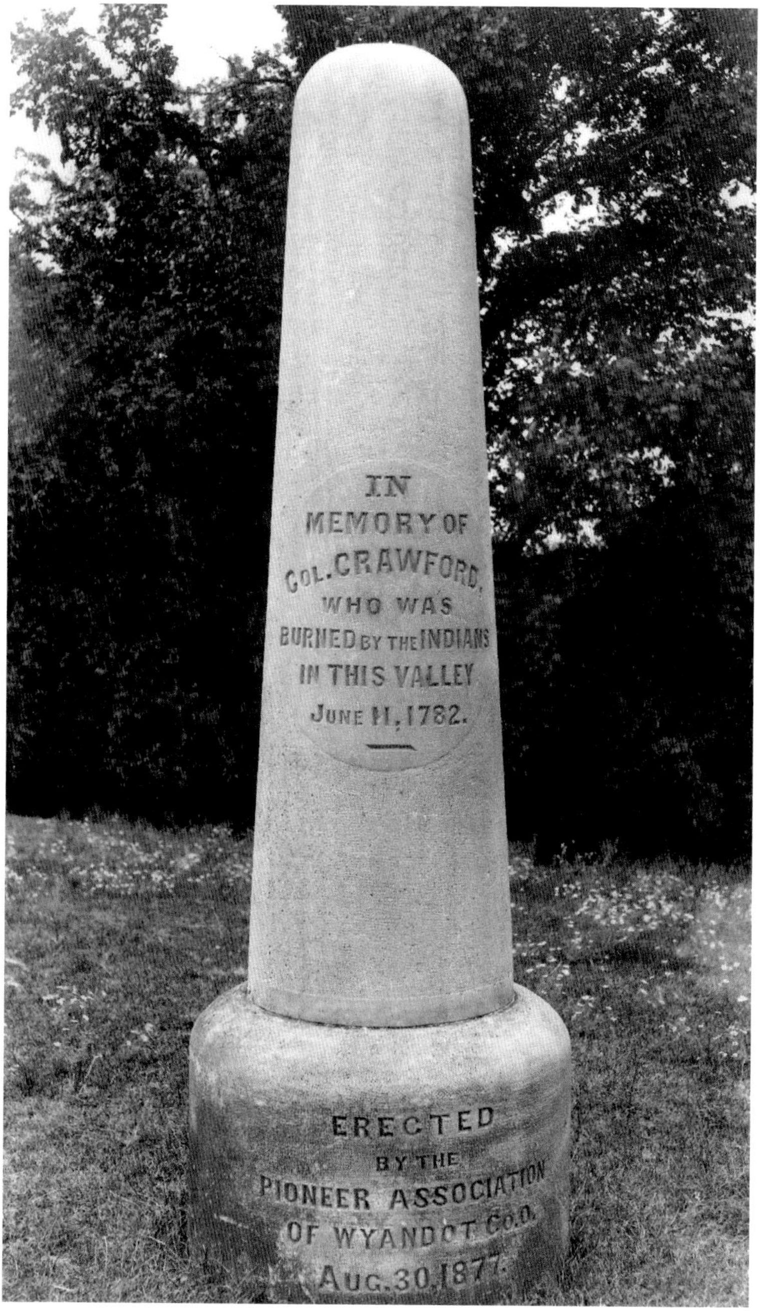

The Pioneer Association of Wyandot County dedicated this sandstone monument to Colonel William Crawford in 1877. It was erected near his suspected execution site. *Wyandot County Historical Society.*

placed in Ritchie Cemetery several hundred yards southwest of the suspected burn site. The new monument was formally dedicated on August 27, 1994, with several hundred persons in attendance.

Preserving the history of Wyandot County and the region was a goal of numerous early residents. There were several failed attempts at starting a historical organization in the early 1900s, and it was not until June 1929 that Charles Artz, Frank Lang and Harry Kinley finally organized the Wyandot County Archaeological and Historical Society.

Shortly after the new association was established, the Wyandot County commissioners secured a small room for the group on the first floor of the courthouse, currently serving as the Law Library. The commissioners also provided the new fledgling Historical Society $600 per year for expenses. As local residents heard of the group, they began loaning items for display in the room, quickly filling it from floor to ceiling. Anything from Native American stone tools and projectile points to pioneer tools to mounted animal specimens and even live turtles were exhibited in the small room.

Many more items were loaned and donated to the organization than could ever be displayed in the limited space. These items were stored in various areas of the courthouse, including the attic and basement. The Wyandot County Museum operated out of the courthouse until moving to the Beery/McConnell House in 1962.

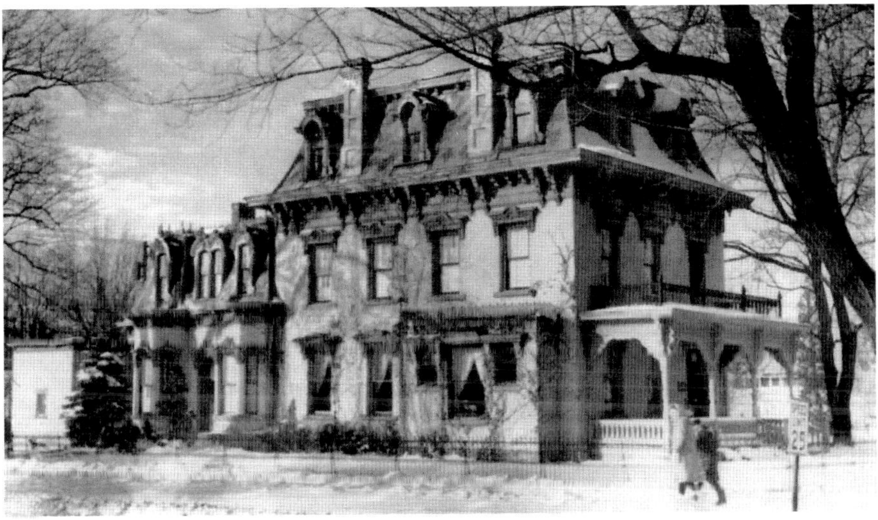

Erected in 1852–53 by George Beery, the Beery/McConnell House was donated by his great-grandson Fowler Beery McConnell for use as the county museum. *Wyandot County Historical Society*.

Fowler Beery McConnell—a great-grandson of George Beery, who built the house in 1852–53—donated the old family home and property to the Wyandot County Archaeological and Historical Society. McConnell inherited the home in 1937 upon his mother's passing. At the time, he was on the board of directors of Sears, Roebuck & Co. and lived in the Chicago area. Not needing the property, the home was soon rented out to relatives. After thirty years with Sears, in 1946, Fowler was named president of the company and became chief executive officer and chairman of the board in 1958. Following his retirement two years later, Fowler, along with his wife, Lucille, donated the old family home in October 1961. Unfortunately, he passed away in December 1961 before the formal dedication of the home. On June 12, 1962, the thirteen-room Wyandot County Museum opened in its new home on Seventh Street.

The museum property also includes the former Maple Grove School from Dunkirk in Hardin County. Originally constructed in 1895, the one-room schoolhouse sat unused on the Keiper farm until donated to the society in 1968. It was restored to its original appearance and opened to the public in 1972. It is used during events and school tours. A railroad shack and a carriage house complete the complex. With ever-changing exhibits, historical events and programs, the site continues to be a source of pride in the local community.

Colonel Joseph McCutchen erected the first building in the new town of McCutchenville, named for him. The Pervain House, now known as the McCutchen Overland Inn, was erected during the summer of 1829. It was originally constructed as a hotel and later served as a stagecoach stop along the Harrison Trail. This was a former Indian trail leading from the Scioto River near Columbus to Lake Erie. It was expanded by General William Henry Harrison during the War of 1812. McCutchen operated his inn until January 1845, when he sold the property to Christopher Pierson.

On October 21, 1845, Pierson sold the land and building to John F. Myers, who operated the Myers Hotel until April 18, 1918, when it was sold at public auction. Hayes Shireman purchased the building and operated it as a boardinghouse and eventually as an apartment building. The Wyandot County Archaeological and Historical Society acquired the building from the Shireman Estate in 1964.

By this time, the structure had become dilapidated and took three years to restore. The fifteen-room McCutchen Overland Inn Museum was dedicated as a stagecoach museum on June 11, 1967, one of only two original stagecoach inn museums known to exist in Ohio. It was returned

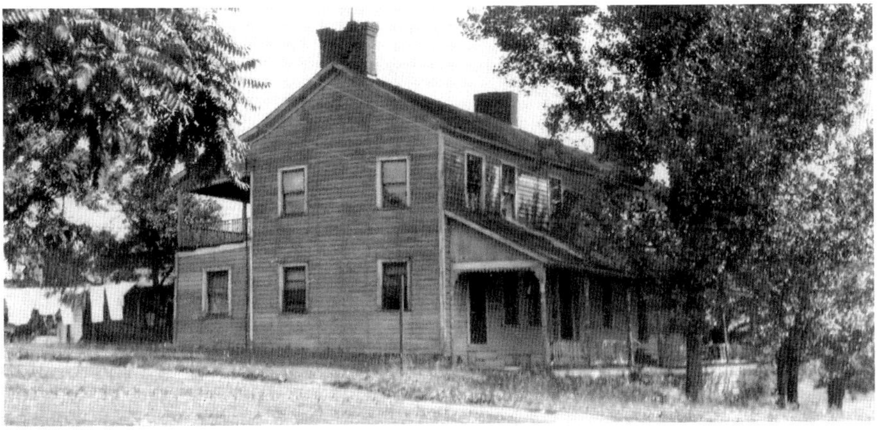

An early twentieth-century view of the McCutchen Overland Inn during its time as the Myers Hotel. It opened as a museum in 1967. *Wyandot County Historical Society.*

to its original appearance and filled with period antiques and furnishings donated by local residents.

Beginning in 2002, a second major renovation turned into a four-year-long restoration project. Over five hundred persons attended the inn's rededication on June 10, 2007. The historic site now includes the Anderson Building, a former general store in McCutchenville and a historic gazebo, which was restored in 2014.

On June 14, 1968, following nearly two years of restoration work, the Ohio Historical Society (now known as the Ohio History Connection) formally opened the Wyandot Indian Mill Museum, the first national museum of milling in a building at its original location. The mill has a long and storied history as detailed in an earlier chapter. After about ten years of ownership, Ward Walton donated the mill to the Ohio Historical Society in 1953. It was not until about a dozen years later that the decision was made to open it as a museum.

A group of men led by John Milligan came out during the summer of 1967 to stabilize and restore the building. During this time, designers and craftsmen were creating visual displays to tell the history of milling in the building. A noted mill historian and author, D.W. Garber, served as consultant on the project and also donated many millwork artifacts, which helped convey the story. Early curators Eula Sanford, Antoinette Lowry and Jean Swebel and maintenance man Harry Shafer also added numerous antiques and historic objects and performed historic research to enhance the visitors' experience. After attracting around one thousand guests at its dedication ceremony, the mill continues to be a great tourist draw in the county.

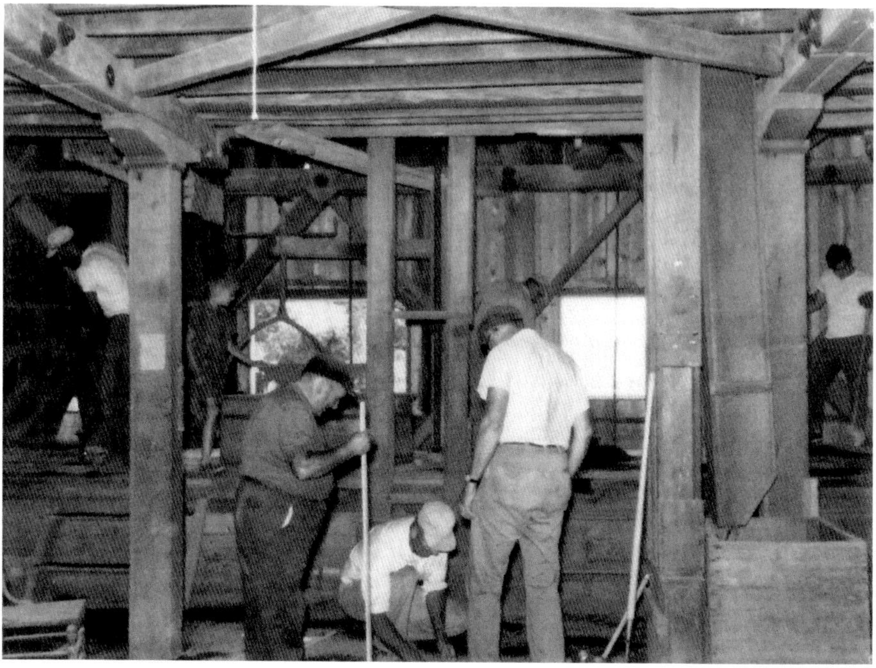

A crew of volunteers led by John Milligan (not pictured) cleaned and repaired the Indian Mill prior to its opening as a museum in 1968. *Wyandot County Historical Society.*

Across the Sandusky River from the mill is the Indian Mill Park, a recreation area officially established in the 1950s but used by local residents since the late 1800s to take advantage of the serene and scenic landscape. On display in the park are the original millstones used by the Wyandottes prior to the erection of the gristmill in 1820. The top stone (runner) was revolved by means of a pole (sweep) operated by two men. It could grind ten to twelve bushels of grain a day. About 1955, Mr. and Mrs. Ward Walton donated the land for the park to the Wyandot County Historical Society. A dedication ceremony featuring Harry Kinley was held on August 25, 1957. During its early years, the park featured a freshwater well for drinking water, public restroom facilities, picnic benches and barbecue grills. Visitors could even camp overnight in the park. After the state acquired the property in the 1980s, it removed many of the physical structures and amenities, opting for a more rustic appearance.

The Wyandot Indian Mill area has seen a large investment by the State of Ohio to attract tourists in recent years. In 2010–11, the Department of Natural Resources and the Ohio Historical Society rebuilt the Indian Mill

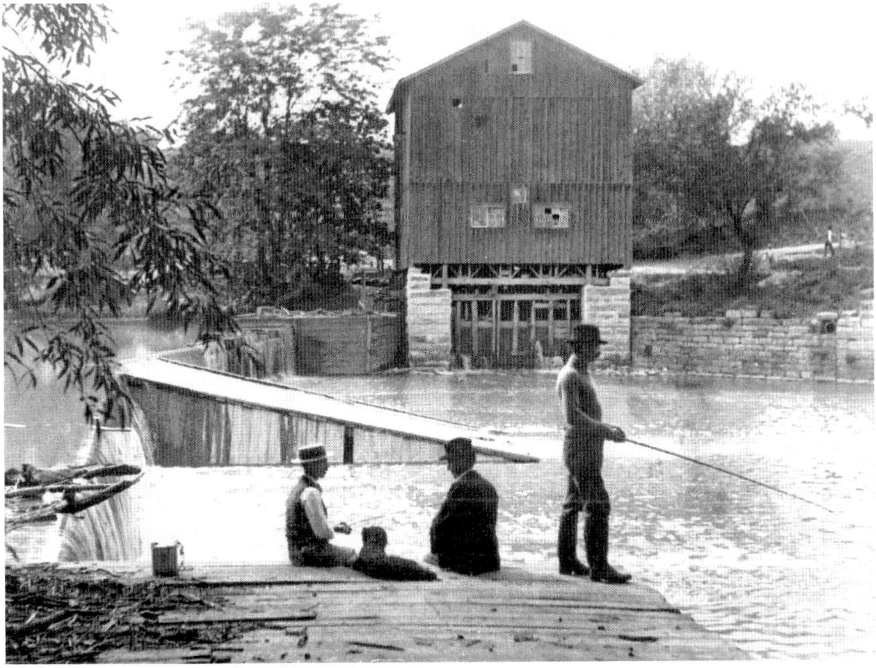

A view of the Indian Mill Dam and fish ladder. The dam across the Sandusky River was originally constructed in 1861 and rebuilt several times. *Wyandot County Historical Society.*

Dam across the Sandusky River. Originally built as a much higher wooden dam to serve the original mills in 1819, it has been lowered and remodeled numerous times, most notably in 1938, 1953 and 1974. During 2013, the ceiling in the Miller's Office was replaced. This same year, the mill's windows were reglazed, several sashes were replaced and repainted and the wooden shutters were restored and rehung.

The Wyandot County commissioners advertised for the "job of building a bridge over the Sandusky River near the Indian Mill" on October 15, 1859. The Indian Mill Covered Bridge was completed in 1861. Additional abutment work was completed by John Tripp in September 1871. To create a new approach to the bridge, the county acquired a half-mile strip of land in May 1872 from David R. Maxwell, operator of the Indian Mill at the time. The bridge served the residents well until March 1913, when the great flood washed it away. Wood from the bridge was salvaged and used to repair numerous bridges damaged in the flood.

In 2014, the Ohio Department of Transportation and the Wyandot County Engineers Department began a project to remove and restore the

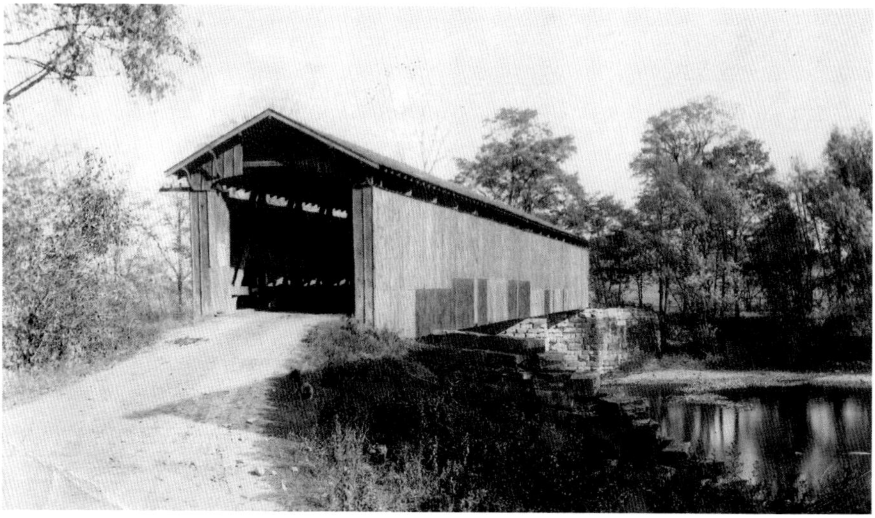

The Indian Mill Covered Bridge was constructed in 1861 and washed away during the Great Flood of 1913, which also flooded the Indian Mill. *Wyandot County Historical Society.*

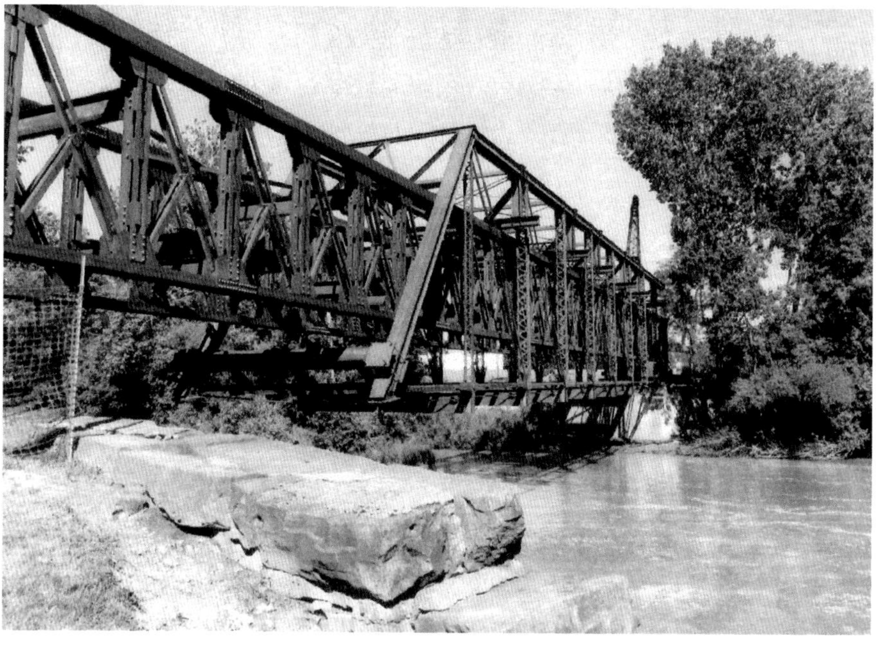

During the 2014–15 restoration project, the removal of the 1913 Indian Mill Cast-Iron Truss Bridge required the use of a pass-through Liberty Bridge. *Wyandot County Historical Society.*

cast-iron Indian Mill Bridge over the Sandusky River. Built by the Modern Construction Company of Fremont in 1913 to replace the original covered bridge that was destroyed earlier in the year, it was in need of maintenance and repair. The 178-foot-long bridge was built with a metal-pinned Pratt through truss construction. A contract was let out for bid, and the United States Bridge Company was selected for the $1.2 million project.

Rather than erect a brand-new bridge at the site, it was decided to dismantle the bridge piece by piece; transport it to the company's workshop in Cambridge, Ohio, where it would be cleaned and regalvanized and its rust spots be removed; and then return it to the original bridge site. A "Liberty Bridge" was constructed through the old bridge, giving the workers a base to operate over the Sandusky River as they dismantled the bridge. During this time, the concrete bases were stabilized and returned to their original appearance. The company began bringing the restored beams back to the site in late 2014. Between December and February 2015, workers reassembled the bridge over the Sandusky River and completed the project in May. While the surrounding park and bridge were being upgraded, the Ohio History Connection began a project to document the interior displays of the Wyandot Indian Mill in preparation for new exhibits to be debuted in 2016.

At one time, Wyandot County had over twenty covered bridges; however, that number is now down to two. The Parker Covered Bridge was built by J.C. Davis in 1873. The single-span Howe through truss bridge crosses the Sandusky River and measures 172 feet long by 16 feet wide. Like many other bridges, it was slightly damaged during the Great Flood of 1913 and was repaired using timbers and boards from the old Indian Mill Bridge.

The structure was set afire by vandals on May 17, 1991, destroying about one-third of it and causing the south end to fall into the river. The Cross Over the Bridge Again Committee was formed to save the bridge and raised $142,000 through a series of fundraisers and obtained a $76,000 grant to pay for its restoration. W.M. Morton Builder, Inc., was hired to construct a replacement bridge, which was dedicated on October 25, 1992.

This was not the last time vandalism struck the bridge. In 1995, a group of local children spray painted graffiti on the bridge, the commemorative plaque and the memorial bricks, which had been sold to raise money for earlier repairs, near the entrance. The offending juveniles were caught and forced to clean off the paint as part of their punishment.

On March 9, 2002, heavy winds as high as eighty miles per hour blew the bridge nearly a foot off its foundation, forcing it to be closed to traffic

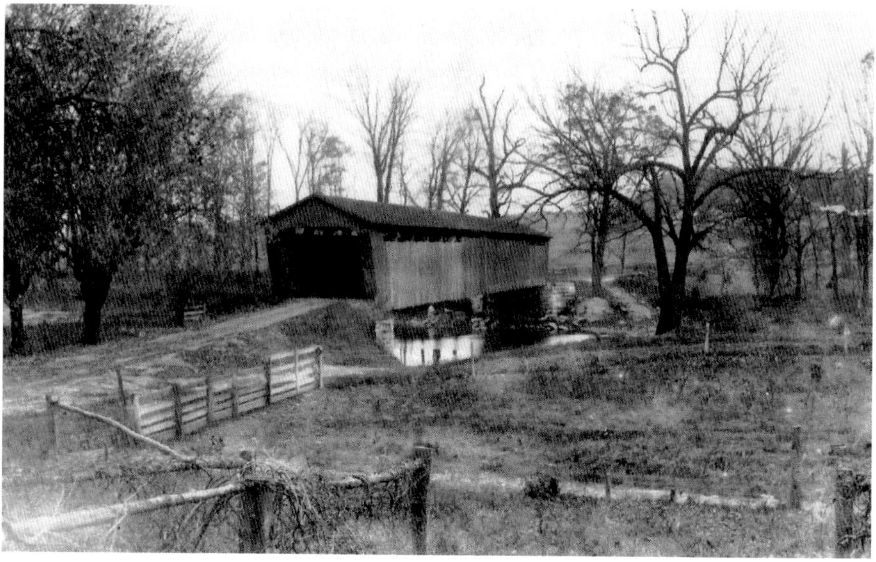

An early 1900s view of the Parker Covered Bridge by Harry Kinley. It was burned in 1991 and restored to its original condition. *Wyandot County Historical Society*.

until repairs were made. Although the damage was covered by the county's insurance, repair estimates were well over $30,000. Remnants of the old restoration committee were still active and donated $2,500 to cover the county's insurance deductible. It has been repaired and still serves the county over 140 years since its opening.

The Swartz Covered Bridge was built in 1878 by Moses Weymouth. The original single-span Howe through truss bridge crossed the Sandusky River and measured 101 feet long by 13 feet wide. The wooden structure sits on sandstone foundation blocks on either side of the river. The bridge was rehabilitated in 1994, reducing its length to 96 feet long. It continues to serve the public nearly 140 years since it was constructed.

As part of Wyandot County's sesquicentennial celebration, a time capsule was placed in the wall at the top of the Wyandot County Courthouse's grand staircase on August 24, 1995, exactly ninety-five years to the day of the building's dedication. Throughout the courthouse are oversized reproductions of Harry Kinley's original photographs placed there as part of the sesquicentennial celebration in 1995.

By the time the courthouse's centennial approached in 1999, the interior paintings had faded and deteriorated so much that the commissioners agreed to restore them. Sandy Bee of Bristol Design Group in Centerville, Ohio,

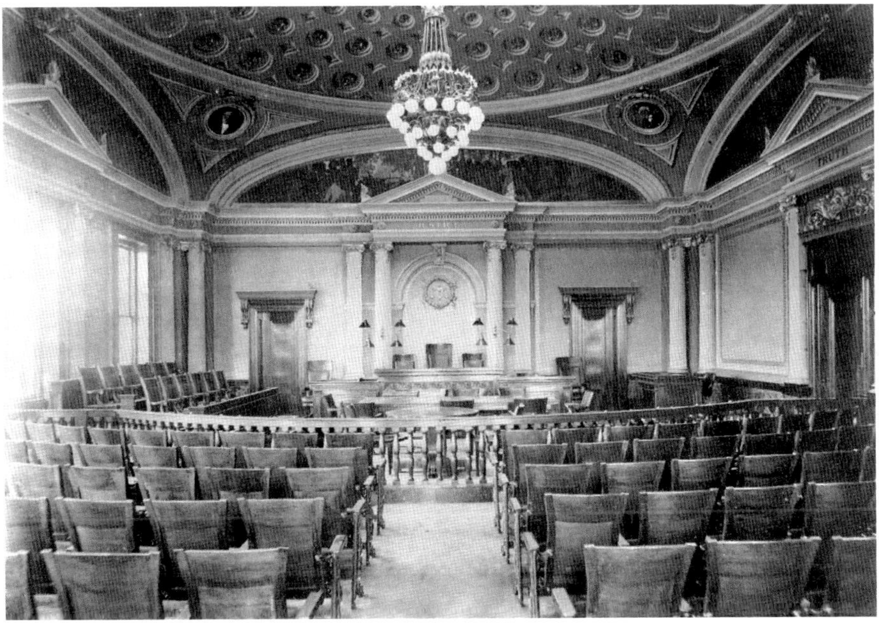

Interior of the third-floor courtroom in the Wyandot County Courthouse. The courtroom, maintained in its original condition, was featured in *The Shawshank Redemption*. *Wyandot County Historical Society*.

was awarded a $116,850 contract to restore the original murals and paintings in the courthouse. Bee also hand-painted new murals for the central dome area that depict the four seasons of spring, summer, fall and winter in the farming community. Work was begun on March 8, 1999, and completed by May 15. New lighting was installed throughout by Vaughn Electric to show off the new paintings.

The following is a description of various decorative elements Bee restored surrounding the stained-glass dome. The medallions represent the seventeen states that existed when Ohio was admitted to the United States in 1803. The four murals (*Mercy*, *Truth*, *Justice* and *Law*) along the upper portion of the walls surrounding the third-floor courtroom tell the history of the Wyandotte Indians. One of these references the death of Colonel Crawford, who was executed by the Delaware Nation in retaliation for the massacre at Gnadenhutten.

The eagle is the national bird of the United States and is found throughout the carvings in the courthouse. Twelve eagles sit in the circle of the dome. The circle symbolizes unity. The outer circle of the dome is a wreath of laurel leaves with its red berries, a symbol of victory and honor. On both sides

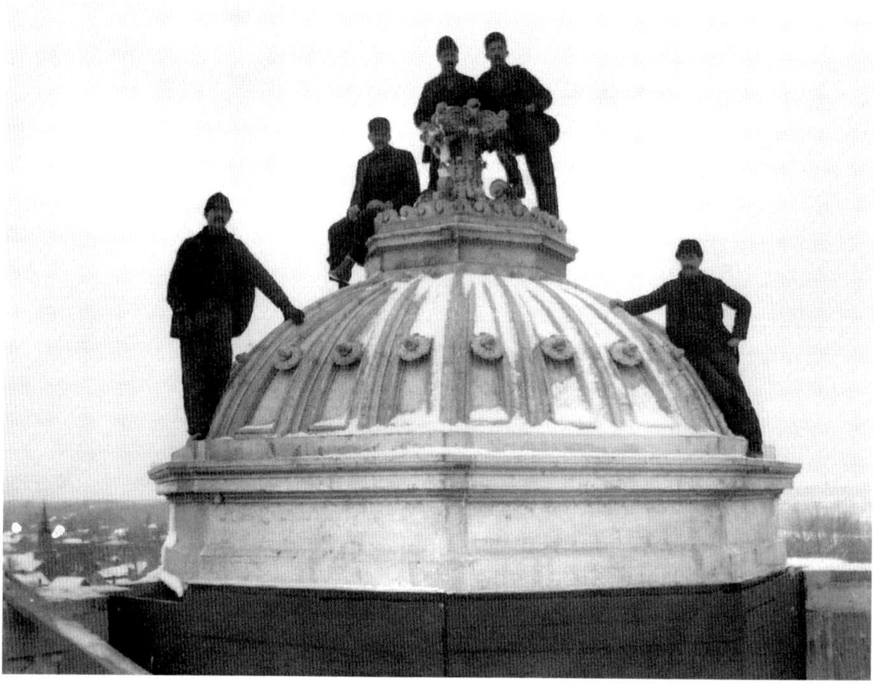

Workers stand on top of the Wyandot County Courthouse's main dome prior to the installation of the statue of *Lady Justice* in 1899. *Wyandot County Historical Society.*

of each eagle is a cascade of entwined flowers. The entwining represents working together. The flowers used are pink and white dogwood (Christian symbol of the wounds of Christ on Calvary), the red rose (the flower of America) and the daisy (the flower of the common man).

During the construction of the new courthouse in 1899, a copper statue of *Lady Justice* was placed on top of the clock tower above the central dome. The statue was manufactured by the W.H. Mullins Company of Salem, Ohio, for $875 and features numerous intricate details (fingernails, eyebrows, braided hair) not visible from its perch 132 feet above the ground.

During the first one hundred plus years of her life, *Lady Justice* suffered numerous "injuries." There were several bullet holes, her scales were blown off during a storm, part of her sword went missing with the rest crudely welded on and a fourteen-inch square section near her hip was completely gone.

The decision was made in the early 2000s to restore the statue. The county commissioners contracted Midstate Construction Company of Marion. In January 2009, the statue was carefully removed for restoration. The final cost of the project was $22,050 with $16,000 donated by the Shawshank Redemption Reunion, a group of locals who served as extras during the filming of the movie in 1993. A time capsule containing numerous local mementoes, including a copy of the video of *The Shawshank Redemption*, was placed inside the statue's skirt before it was replaced on the courthouse. Upon completion, *Lady Justice* was slowly hoisted back to her place of honor overlooking the county on June 8, 2009.

Not only had the interior of the structure and *Lady Justice* suffered damage, but the elements had also taken their toll on the domes and exterior roofline. By the 2010s, the damage inside and outside the domes was so bad that something needed to be done to save the building. Due to a lack of available funds for the project, the best option was a tax levy. The Wyandot County Courthouse Restoration Association was formed and held several events to raise awareness and support of the levy. County voters overwhelmingly approved a six-year bond issue in November 2013 that will generate roughly $2.5 million for the courthouse restoration. The funds are to be allocated for only structural improvements to the roof, not for interior work. Some of the items to be addressed are the leaking roof, crumbling concrete and steel supports, corroded copper gutters and damaged domes.

A contract was signed on August 21, 2014, with Midstate Contractors Inc., which had previously worked on *Lady Justice* and was familiar with the structure. Work began in late 2014 and is expected to last about two years.

The local community's good relationship with the Wyandotte Nation—evidenced by all the Wyandotte-related sites located in the county—is something it is extremely proud of. Over the years, numerous Wyandottes from the Wyandotte Nation of Oklahoma, Wyandot Nation of Kansas, Wyandot Nation of Anderdon (Michigan) and Huron-Wendat Nation of Wendake in Canada have journeyed to their ancestral homeland. During the 2010s, high school and college interns from the Wyandotte Nation in Oklahoma returned to walk in the footsteps of and learn about their ancestors. In 2014, a group of Wyandotte seniors visited the county, many for the first time, to tour the sites associated with the Grand Reserve. It is a great honor to have the opportunity to share the cultural history of the Wyandottes with them and the general public.

Tribal leaders such as Chief Leonard Cotter, Chief Leaford Bearskin, Chief Billy Friend, Chief Ted Roll and Chief Janith English have met and shared stories with local historians since the 1970s. Both sides have learned much about the past and are working toward a common goal: preserving their shared heritage. After all, one cannot truly tell the story of Wyandot

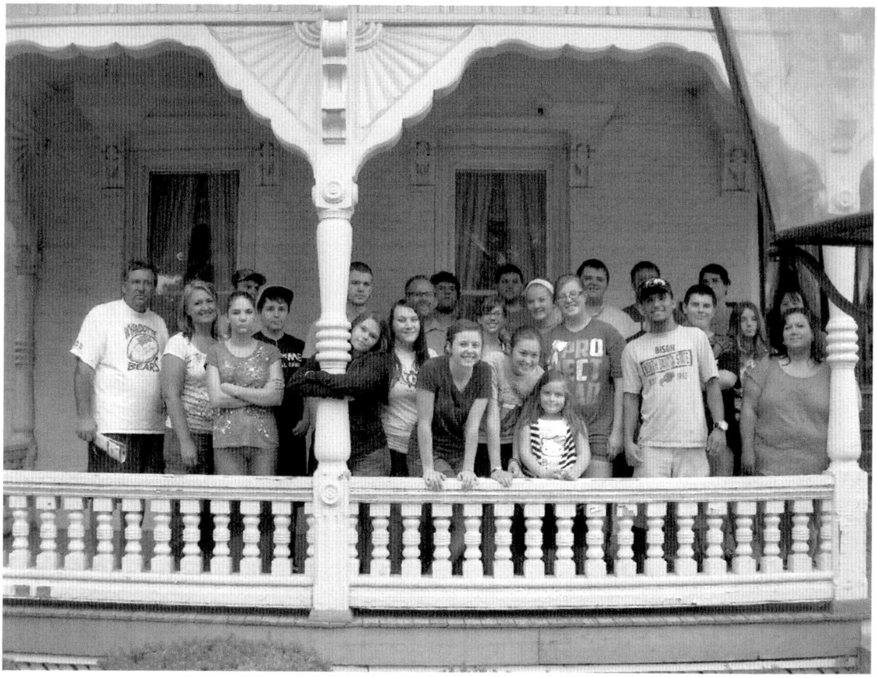

Interns from the Wyandotte Nation of Oklahoma visited the Wyandot County Museum during their trip to Wyandot County in the summer of 2012. *Wyandot County Historical Society.*

County without first including the story of the Wyandotte Nation. New exhibits and celebrations are planned across Wyandot County in 2016, the 200th anniversary of the arrival of John Stewart and the birth of Mother Solomon. Over the next ten years, residents will observe the 200th anniversary of the Wyandotte Reservations, the Indian Mill and the Mission Church. This will be a time to honor the past while looking toward the future.

Bibliography

Atlas of Wyandot County, Ohio. Philadelphia: Harrison and Hare, 1879.

Baughman, Abraham J., ed. *Past and Present of Wyandot County, Ohio*. Chicago: S.J. Clarke Publishing Company, 1913.

Biographical Memoirs of Wyandot County, Ohio. Logansport, IN: B.F. Bowen, 1902.

Borentz, Eileen Kirkwood. *And They Called It Carey*. Carey, OH: Carey Progressor-Times, 1993.

Bowen, Jeb E., ed. "Ancient Population Stability." *Wyandot County Archaeology* 1 (1988): 2.

———. "Current Status of Wyandot County Prehistory." *Wyandot County Archaeology* 1 (1988): 2.

———. "The 'Glacial Kame' People." *Wyandot County Archaeology* 1 (1988): 1.

———. "Original Vegetation Based on Government Land Office Surveys." *Wyandot County Archaeology* 1 (1988): 1.

Butterfield, C.W. *An Historical Account of the Expedition Against Sandusky Under Col. William Crawford in 1782*. Cincinnati, OH: Robert Clark and Company, 1873.

Carey, Ohio. Carey, OH: Carey Progressor-Times, 2008.

Cash, Paula. *100th Anniversary Pioneer Log Cabin Upper Sandusky, Ohio (1888–1988)*. Upper Sandusky, OH: Wyandot County Historical Society, 1988.

Darabont, Frank, director. *The Shawshank Redemption*. DVD. West Hollywood, CA: Castle Rock Entertainment, Inc., 1994.

Dickens, Charles. *American Notes for General Circulation*. London: Chapman and Hall, 1842.

Finley, Anthony. *General Atlas*. Philadelphia: Finley, 1828.

Finley, Reverend James B. *History of the Wyandot Mission at Upper Sandusky, Ohio*. Cincinnati, OH: John F. Wright and Leroy Swormstedt, 1840.

First Annual Directory of Sycamore Village. Sycamore, OH: F. Ladd, 1889.

Galitza, Edward. "Ceremonialism as Practiced by the Glacial Kame Culture." *Ohio Archaeologist* 20 (1970): 204–05.

———. "Glacial Kame Artifacts." *Ohio Archaeologist* 6 (1957): 140–41.

Galitza, Edward, and Norman L. Dunn. "Glacial Kame Evidence in Wyandot County." *Ohio Archaeologist* 6 (1956): 7–10.

Gottfried, Ray D. *Pictorial Memories: Upper Sandusky & Wyandot County*. Upper Sandusky, OH: Ray D. Gottfried, 1976.

Helwig, Richard M., and Richard N. Helwig. *Ghost Towns of Wyandot County, Issue 32*. Sunbury, OH: Center for Ghost Town Research in Ohio, 2001.

Hill, Leonard U. *John Johnson and the Indians: In the Land of the Three Miamis*. Piqua, OH: Leonard U. Hill, 1957.

Hill, Tom, and Ashley Peyton. *Images of America: Upper Sandusky*. Mount Pleasant, SC: Arcadia Publishing, 2010.

Hill, Tom, and Marnie Hill. *Images of America: Wyandot County*. Mount Pleasant, SC: Arcadia Publishing, 2011.

The History of Crawford County and Ohio. Chicago: Baskin and Battey, 1881.

The History of Wyandot County, Ohio. Chicago: Leggett, Conaway and Company, 1884.

Howe, Henry. *Historical Collections of Ohio in Three Volumes*. Columbus, OH: Henry Howe and Son, 1891.

"Inductees." Wyandot County Sports Hall of Fame. http://www.wyandotsportshof.org.

Kappler, Charles J., ed. *Indian Affairs: Laws and Treaties*. Vol. 2, *Treaties*. Washington, D.C.: Government Printing Office, 1904.

Lawrence, David, ed. *Indian Village Volume LIX*. Upper Sandusky, OH: Upper Sandusky High School, 1970.

Lima News. "Tragedy Near Kenton Airline's 1st—Lake Central Crash Claims 38." March 3, 1967.

Lincoln Highway Association Inc. *The Complete Official Road Guide of the Lincoln Highway*. 5th ed. Detroit: Lincoln Highway Association Inc., 1924.

Marsh, Thelma. *Daughter of Grey Eyes: The Story of Mother Solomon*. Upper Sandusky, OH: United Methodist Historical Society, 1984.

———. *Lest We Forget: A Brief Sketch of Wyandot County's History*. Upper Sandusky, OH: Thelma Marsh, 1977.

———. *Moccasin Trails to the Cross: A History of the Mission to the Wyandot Indians on the Sandusky Plains*. Upper Sandusky, OH: United Methodist Historical Society, 1974.

Mills, William C. *Archaeological Atlas of Ohio*. Columbus, OH: Fred J. Heer, 1914.

Mitchell, Joseph. *The Missionary Pioneer; or, A Brief Memoir of the Life, Labours, and Death of John Stewart (Man of Colour)*. New York: J.C. Totten, 1827.

Mohr, Kim Dysinger. *Echoes Along the Sandusky: Tales from Our Forefathers*. Sycamore, OH: Mohawk Historical Society, 2009.

Moore's Standard Directory of Upper Sandusky 1908–1909. Upper Sandusky, OH: S.H. Moore Company, 1908.

National Transportation Safety Board. *Aircraft Accident Report: Propeller Separation, Lake Central Airlines, Inc., Allison Prop-Jet Convair 340, N73130, Near Marseilles, Ohio, March 5, 1967*. Washington, D.C.: United States Department of Transportation, 1968.

The New Directory and History of Nevada. Nevada, OH: Superior Printing Company, 1894.

Ohio High School Athletic Association. http://www.ohsaa.org.

"Ohio's Trail of Tears." Wyandotte Nation. http://www.wyandotte-nation.org.

Pocket Directory of Upper Sandusky, Ohio. Upper Sandusky, OH: Wyandot Democratic Union Print Shop, 1880.

Saumenig Directory Company's Upper Sandusky City Directory and Wyandot County Gazetteer. Marion, IN: Saumenig Directory Company, 1915.

Terry, Joe. "I'll Take Potpourri for a Thousand, Alex." *Bottles and Extras* 17 (2006): 2–6.

The Union. "The Old Mission—Its Reconstruction and Rededication Last Saturday." September 24, 1889.

The Upper Sandusky Folklore Class of 1983. *1953–1983: The Red Slipper Murder Case Thirty Years Later*. Upper Sandusky, OH: Wyandot County Historical Society, 1983.

"The 'U.S.' Model A Gasoline Runabout." *Cycle and Automobile Trade Journal* 12 (1907): 68.

"U.S. Motor Cars." *Cycle and Automobile Trade Journal* 12 (1907): 146.

VetFriends. https://www.vetfriends.com/index.cfm.

Vogel, John J. *Indians of Ohio and Wyandot County*. New York: Vantage Press, 1975.

Watts, Arethusa. *Mostly Ghosts: Stagecoach Inns, Hotels, Covered Bridges, and Towns in Wyandot County Ohio*. Upper Sandusky, OH: Wyandot County Genealogy Society, 1985.

Wheeler, Reverend James. *Diary of a Methodist Circuit Rider 1857*. Upper Sandusky, OH: Wyandot County Historical Society, n.d.

Winter, Nevin O., ed. *A History of Northwest Ohio*. Chicago: Lewis Publishing Company, 1917.

Wyandot County Directory. Upper Sandusky, OH: Gillingham and Talcott, 1877.

Wyandot Tracers, OGS. *Pictorial Memories of One-Room Schools in Wyandot County, Ohio (1885–1930)*. Upper Sandusky, OH: Wyandot County Genealogy Society, 1995.

———. *School Bells Ringing Out Our Heritage: Early Schools of Wyandot Co., Ohio*. Upper Sandusky, OH: Wyandot County Genealogy Society, 1988.

Index

K

L

M

N

O

About the Author

Ronald I. Marvin Jr. is the director of the Wyandot County Archaeological and Historical Society and curator of the Wyandot County Museum. A veteran of the U.S. Army, he served in Operation Desert Shield and Operation Desert Storm with the First Infantry Division. Marvin has been involved with museums and archaeological laboratories across the county for over twenty-five years, beginning in high school. He holds a bachelor of arts in history and anthropology from the University of South Dakota and a master of arts in museum studies from the University of Nebraska. The author currently lives in Kenton, Ohio, and has researched, written and lectured extensively about Wyandot and Hardin Counties.

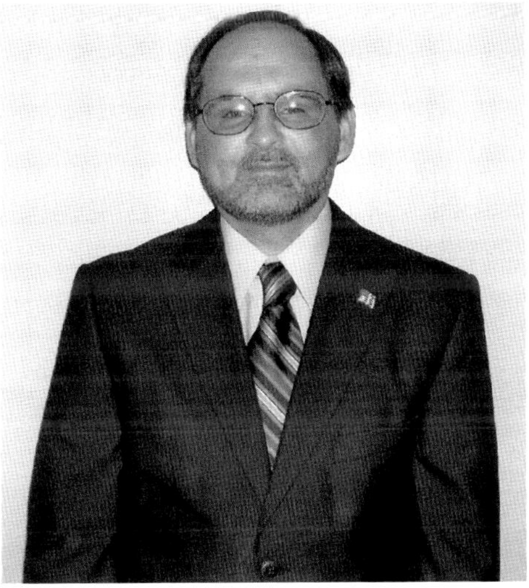

Author's collection.